The Wound of Knowledge

ROWAN WILLIAMS

The Wound of Knowledge

Christian Spirituality from the New Testament to St John of the Cross

Darton, Longman & Todd
London

First published in Great Britain in 1979
Darton, Longman & Todd Ltd
89 Lillie Road
London SW6 1UD

Printed in Great Britain by The Anchor Press Ltd
and bound by Wm Brendon & Son Ltd
both of Tiptree, Essex

ISBN 0 232 51425 9

Contents

Preface

This book grew out of four years' experience of lecturing on the history of Christian spirituality, first at the College of the Resurrection, Mirfield, then at Westcott House, Cambridge; to all the students who listened, criticized and discussed, my debt is very great indeed. Without their responsiveness and intelligent sympathy, this book would never have been written. I must also express my gratitude to the Community of the Resurrection for first inviting me to lecture on this subject at Mirfield and for providing so congenial and supportive an environment to live and work in. I am no less indebted to my colleagues and associates in Cambridge for faithful friendship and consistent stimulation. Canon Mark Santer, Principal of Westcott, and Dr Nicholas Lash, Norris-Hulse Professor of Divinity, have both contributed more than they perhaps realize to these pages.

My thanks also to the Benedictine community of Downside Abbey for inviting me to talk to their novitiate on some of the subjects here dealt with. Dom Illtyd Trethowan of Downside has given generously of his time over many years to discussions of theology, philosophy and spirituality: I look back with great delight on the hours spent in his company.

The Sisters of the Love of God at Fairacres have given me unflagging support by friendship and prayers since my student days. I am very specially grateful to Sister Benedicta Ward, and (like so many others) to Mother Mary Clare; both have shown me so much of the courage and the costly honesty that go with genuine spiritual vision and maturity.

I have had great help from being able to read transcripts of several lectures given in Oxford by the Revd Andrew Louth of Worcester College on Greek Mystical Theology: the scope and sensitivity of his patristic scholarship are both an inspiration and a reproach to an amateur like myself. The Revd John Saward, now of Tregony in Cornwall, has shared with me his reflections on many aspects of the history of spirituality, and I have never spoken with him without learning something fresh and being shown some new facet of a familiar subject.

Two people have perhaps done more than any others to direct my thoughts and prayers for the last nine or ten years: Dom Joseph Warrilow of Quarr Abbey and Professor Donald MacKinnon, Norris-Hulse Professor Emeritus in the University of Cambridge. What I owe to these men is not easily expressible, and I must be content with this barest of acknowledgements to voice my love, respect and gratitude.

I hope that all those who have thus contributed to this work will look with their usual charity on its many imperfections, to which they have contributed nothing.

Last, but far from least, my heartfelt thanks to my mother for heroically volunteering to type the manuscript and producing so expert and professional a result. An author's problems are immeasurably reduced by such help; and by publishers as efficient, friendly and sympathetic as the staff of Darton, Longman and Todd.

The title is drawn from a recent poem by R. S. Thomas (who has long since said most of what I want to say), 'Roger Bacon', in *Frequencies* (London, Macmillan, 1978), p. 40.

Rowan Williams
Petertide, 1979

1. The Passion of My God

Christian faith has its beginnings in an experience of profound contradictoriness, an experience which so questioned the religious categories of its time that the resulting reorganization of religious language was a centuries-long task. At one level, indeed, it is a task which every generation has to undertake again. And if 'spirituality' can be given any coherent meaning, perhaps it is to be understood in terms of this task: each believer making his or her own that engagement with the questioning at the heart of faith which is so evident in the classical documents of Christian belief. This is *not,* it must be said, to recommend any of the currently fashionable varieties of relativism or to romanticize a wistful 'half-belief'. The questioning involved here is not our interrogation of the data, but its interrogation of us. It is the intractable *strangeness* of the ground of belief that must constantly be allowed to challenge the fixed assumptions of religiosity; it is a *given*, whose question to each succeeding age is fundamentally one and the same. And the greatness of the great Christian saints lies in their readiness to be questioned, judged, stripped naked and left speechless by that which lies at the centre of their faith.

The problem was, is and always will be the Christian attitude to the historical order, the human past. By affirming that all 'meaning', every assertion about the significance of life and reality, must be judged by reference to a brief succession of contingent events in Palestine, Christianity – almost without realizing it – closed off the path to 'timeless truth'. That is to say, it becomes increasingly difficult in the Christian world to see the ultimately important human experience as an escape into the transcendent, a flight out of history and the flesh. Even when Christian writers use language suggesting such a picture, there are strong forces pulling in an opposite direction, demanding the affirmation of history, and thus of human change and growth, as significant. If the heart of 'meaning' is a human story, a story of growth, conflict and death, every human story, with all its oddity and ambivalence, becomes open to interpretation in terms of God's saving work. Once we have stopped drawing a distinction between 'compromising' activities and spheres (the family, the state, the individual body or psyche) and 'pure' realities (the soul, the intelligible world), the spiritual life becomes a much more complex, demanding and far-reaching matter. 'Spirituality' becomes far more than a science of interpreting exceptional private experiences; it must now touch every area of human experience, the public and social, the painful, negative, even pathological byways of the mind, the moral and relational world. And the goal of a Christian life becomes not enlightenment but wholeness – an acceptance of this complicated and muddled bundle of experiences as a possible theatre for God's creative work.

The pages which follow are meant as an introduction to the ways in which a succession of Christian saints attempted to articulate their vision of the Christian calling, the diverse ways in which they responded to the call towards wholeness. In the life and work of each of them, we may see the conflict and puzzlement which follow inevitably from the nature of their data. But it is a conflict supported and made bearable by one thing: every Christian thinker, if he or she at all merits the designation, begins from the experience of being reconciled, being accepted, being held (however precariously) in the grace of God. And this is mediated in the objective form of a shared life and language, a public and historical community of men and women, gathering to read certain texts and perform certain acts. That which transmits God's question from generation to generation is the Church (perhaps the Church can be defined only in some such way, as the bearer of that question; and, conversely, it might be said that whatever bears that question is, or is within, the Church);

in this vastly diverse community, extending so widely in time and space, are the first resources for each person to live with the question. The failure of *every* Christian to grasp and express the fullness of God's act in history can itself be a sustaining, even a heartening witness to our own particular doubts. The sense of common enterprise, *shared* speech, may help to save the individual, if only by reminding him or her that the focus of meaning is not private and particular, but a reality which incorporates and gives an identity and a structure to individual experience, and is never reducible to its limited terms. The study of the Christian past should properly be an exercise in living more seriously *in* the Church and *into* the historical corporateness of its tradition – not passively or uncritically, but with enough commitment to find it in nourishment and hope.

The first question, then, must be about the nature of our datum itself, the nature of God's alleged presence and work in Palestine. More specifically still, we must turn our attention to that aspect of the story of God-in-Christ which most sharply focuses the problems posed here for religious language. The final control and measure and irritant in Christian speech remains the cross: the execution of Jesus of Nazareth. Christianity is born out of struggle because it is born from men and women faced with the paradox of God's purpose made flesh in a dead and condemned man. Without the cross there would be no New Testament. Those who at first believed in Jesus of Nazareth as God's herald and delegate had to resolve the appalling paradox that the fulfiller of God's Law had been condemned and killed by the people of God under the Law of God. The new age of the Messiah had dawned in the slaughter of the Messiah at the instigation of the Messianic people. Now this has little to do with the scholar's problem of how far exactly the Jewish courts were legally responsible for Jesus' death, still less with the absurdity (far too belatedly disowned by the Christian Church) of talking about a continuing 'responsibility' of the Jewish people for it. What is at issue is that the first Christians were painfully aware that God's chosen one and God's chosen people had come into open and tragic conflict: that God seemed to be set against God. If God is to be seen at work here, he is indeed a strange God, a hidden God, who does not uncover his will in a straight line of development, but fully enters into a world of confusion and ambiguity and works in contradictions – the new covenant which both fulfils and radically alters the old, the Messianic age made real amid the suffering and failure of the present time.

New Testament Foundations

It is the experience of these tensions which underlies most of the writings of the New Testament. In one way or another, practically all the writers are attempting to come to terms with the devastating finality of the life and death of Jesus: a finality which, on the one hand, means that attitudes to the law and the chosen people cannot ever be the same again and, on the other, leaves the believer with all the problems of living in a visibly untransformed world. Yet the finality is inescapable. The believer now lives in and from the life of Jesus crucified and *risen*. The dead Jesus has been vindicated by his Father: the resurrection is that which *points to* the crucified as God's decisive manifestation. He is 'designated Son of God in power according to the Spirit of holiness by his resurrection from the dead' (Rom. 1.4); 'God has highly exalted him and bestowed on him the name which is above every name' (Phil. 2.9). Now that he is risen, the reconciliation he brings is made available for all men in all times and places (Matt. 28. 18–20, Luke 24. 45–8, John 20. 21–3). He is no longer limited by his historical particularity (no longer known 'from a human point of view', 'after the flesh' – 2 Cor. 5.16), though he never ceases to *be* particular – the man executed under Pontius Pilate, and no other. He does not belong to a finished and determined past, not even physically, as the stories of the empty grave impress upon us. He is 'Lord'. All things, all conditions, are now to be referred to him, to the pattern set by his story. And it is in this sense that Jesus alters the past of Judaism as well as the present of the believer. The resurrection, which sets free the mission of the Church to reconcile, which *creates* reconciled lives, directs us to Calvary as an event which uncovers the truth, the resilient, inexhaustible, demanding objectivity of what God and God's work is like. From now on, all that can be said of God's action in the past or the present must pass under the judgement of this fact.

One immediate and disturbing implication of this is that God provokes crisis and division. Even during his ministry, Jesus had regularly spoken of the tragically divisive nature of his work (Matt. 10. 34–9 and parallels, 23. 37–9 and parallels and, most starkly, 26.24 and parallels): the Fourth Gospel makes this a major literary theme, employing unparalleled subtlety in underlining the inexorable ironies of salvation and condemnation united in a single story. But it is Paul, especially in Romans and 2 Corinthians, who makes perhaps the most serious attempt in the New Testament to face and understand this. The ninth to the eleventh chapters of Romans painfully confront the question, of such personal urgency to Paul himself, of God's fidelity and consistency. Has the word of God failed? Is God unjust? Has he rejected his people? These queries send the reader back to the bleakest pages of the Old Testament – Lamentations, Job, the terrible eighty-ninth Psalm: God is the one who rejects and destroys, not only the one who elects and loves. He *drives* his people into turning their backs upon him; there are echoes of that hard Johannine saying, 'If I had not come and spoken to them, they would not have sin' (John 15.22). The rejection of Jesus by men is at the same time the rejection of men by God, and it is acted out among the particular people whose privilege and burden it is to understand the intimacy of election to the full. Paul is here pointing to the single but enormous fact which forced Christianity out of its Jewish milieu, which made, and makes, Christian belief distinctively itself. It is not an ascription of 'importance' to Jesus, not even a recognition of him as a supreme directive teacher or example. It is the acknowledgement of God as a God who is present in and works in human failure and helplessness – so much so that it can be said that he 'forces' men into a decision to acknowledge or not to acknowledge their failure, in the events of Jesus' life and death.

God reveals the inadequacy of Law in the death of Jesus.

'Law', in one sense or another, is what brings Jesus to death, what cannot allow him to coexist with it. And, for Paul, 'Law' is most fundamentally self-dependence. The bitter paradox in the history of Israel is that the Torah, which is a means of grace, has become the great impediment to grace (Rom. 9.30–3), a truth which, again, Jesus' own preaching reflects (Matt. 23.13). And it is Jesus' death which, dramatically and extremely, unmasks 'Law' for what it is: the refusal of grace, of reconciliation, of the Kingdom, by people who will not acknowledge their neediness or, in Johannine terms, their blindness (John. 8.41). Without the experience of grace, we live by 'Law', by the accumulation of patterns of behaviour, plans and projects and organizations of our life; and God can and does work through this, in all its ambivalence. But Christ – and Christ *crucified* – proclaims the ultimate irrelevance of pattern and project. We have struggled to build a secure reality resting on our individual subjectivities; but the only secure reality is something almost absurdly different, the anarchic mercy of God, which ignores order, rank and merit. And that is something which Law, of its nature, cannot bear. So it is that the proclamation of unconditional compassion meets with drastic rejection: to believe in Jesus' God is to recognize that our projects and patterns are the marks of failure and illusion and the childish belief that we can dictate truth and reality; and if we cannot accept our failure, we can at least try to obliterate the light which has made it clear to us. Only such a total collision – the utter rejection of unconditional love – can uncover what it is that we are *really* doing in living under Law. God provokes crisis to destroy our self-deceiving trust in Law; our dependence upon what we as individuals can make and sustain is what cuts us off from any reality in the selfhood we so treasure. Self-dependence is the subtlest mechanism of self-destruction, and to cling to it in the face of grace is a thinly veiled self-hatred.

'God has consigned all men to disobedience, that he may have mercy upon all' (Rom. 11.32), writes Paul; and, 'the scripture consigned all things to sin, that what was promised to faith in Jesus Christ might be given to those who believe' (Gal. 3.22). The continuity and unity of God's work is, for Paul, manifest in these extraordinary reversals; and of course it is not easy for Paul, any more than for any believer, to assimilate this. At the conclusion of all the involved rabbinical disputation of Romans 9 to 11, he can do no more than cry out his wonder at the ways of God. It is a wonder not entirely new in Scripture; by some providential accident, it is Psalm 89, with its agonized protests, which concludes the third book of the Psalter and so ends with the doxology, 'Blessed be the LORD for ever! Amen and Amen.' But Paul has been compelled to examine the logic of the greatest rejection of all, to strive for a reconciliation of his most basic commitments. He believes in God's election of Israel; in Israel as the paradigmatic recipient of grace; in God's self-consistency and faithfulness to his promises; and in God's decisive presence and work in the crucified Jesus, and his election of those baptized into Jesus. A god who can be the object of such commitment is a God who saves by fire. Conversion and repentance – those words which Christians of all persuasions have come to use so glibly – involve going down into the chaotic waters of Christ's death, so that the Spirit can move to make 'new creation'; being unmade to be remade.

It is part of the whole logic of this argument that the new life is not simply infused in all-conquering fullness in a single moment. It does not become a new Law, a new fixed pattern or possession, but a new state of affairs, the new 'position' in which the believer can address the Father as Jesus had done, as 'Abba' (Rom. 8.15, Gal. 4.6), a new state above all of *liberty* (2 Cor. 3.17), but never a state possessed, always one *to be* realized. The Spirit is given as pledge, 'advance payment' (2 Cor. 5.5), as the ground of hope; and life in the Spirit is a 'straining forward to what lies ahead' (Phil. 3.13). The Spirit's work is to make the believer like Christ, and being like Christ means *living through* certain kinds of human experience – not once, but daily. The second letter to the Corinthians is Paul's most passionate meditation on this. Here he speaks of the daily affliction, the daily rejection, the daily dying by which the Spirit works, transforming us 'from one degree of glory to another' (3.18). The veil of the Law is removed, illusion is stripped away; but only slowly does this penetrate every area of human living. And it penetrates by means of the pervasive and inexorable experience of failure, by the 'wasting away' (4.16) of the instincts which look for clarity, ease and effectiveness and the acceptance of the hiddenness of God's working. God's servants, writes Paul with a delighted irony, have to 'commend themselves' by their disasters, 'in ill repute and good repute', acknowledging the flat paradoxicality of the believer's life in the eyes of the world (6. 3–10). And although the later chapters of this epistle most probably come from a different document, it was a sound instinct which united them with the beginning. For here Paul in grief and anger and bitterness spreads out his apostolic credentials to the sceptical: a catalogue of wretchedness, concluding with the humiliating memory of his ignominious escape from Damascus (11. 32–3). Here is the transfiguration from glory to glory, realized daily in the absurd, the bitter, even the comical; this is, surprisingly, what it is to live in the Messianic age and be conformed to the pattern of the Messiah. When the future breaks into the present order, it shows itself in Paul's 'folly' for Christ, in the stupid incongruities of this curious life in two worlds.

The new life is not a possession. It is, simply, new *life* – that is to say, a new world of possibilities, a new future which is to be constructed day by day. Life, after all, implies movement and growth. And perhaps this rather banal and obvious point is an indicator of what must be central for any adequate understanding of Christian spirituality. It is worth noting how much stress not only Paul but other writers lay upon the themes of the call to maturity and the risks of regression: salvation is to be realized in growth, and not to grow is to fall away. The opening chapters of 1 Corinthians remind a community of self-satisfied and factious converts that they are chosen in the first place for their weakness (1. 26–31) and that their calling is to an ever greater identification with the weakness and hiddenness of God's action in Christ (1. 17–25, 2. 1–9); and this (2.6) is their maturity and their wisdom – a maturity which their various self-assertions amply show them not to possess (3. 1–4). They believe themselves to have entered securely upon an inheritance; and Paul expends some of his heaviest sarcasm upon this confidence (4. 8–13). They are confident of their spiritual riches, they measure their growth in terms of tangible spiritual acquisition; but God marks out his servants by their constant humiliations, 'as the refuse of the world, the offscouring of all things' (4.13). As much as in 2 Corinthians, Paul is struggling against a view which sees growth as achievement, a 'thing' acquired; for this has nothing to do with his own sense of being daily grasped in his helplessness by a totally demanding and transforming fact, the death, and life past death, of Jesus the Messiah.

So much is this a whole and finished reality over against him that he has small interest in the imitation of Jesus' life. It would be wholly wrong to say that he has no 'imitation' spirituality; but what is involved, what is to be followed, is the single great fact of obedience and self-emptying – Christ who 'though he was rich, yet for your sake . . . became poor, so that by his poverty you might become rich' (2 Cor. 8.9). And as the significance of Christ grows more and more plain, and the language of pre-existence and cosmic lordship begins to appear, so, proportionately, does the sense of wonder at the scale of humility and poverty involved in Jesus' life and death. The greatest statement of this is, of course, the Christological hymn of Philippians 2, with its eloquent echoes of the gospel's concern with the redeemer as servant or slave of all. But this is not the only response to the event of Christ's death among the early writers. The writer to the Hebrews is no less concerned than Paul with maturity and regression (Heb. 5.11 – 6.12, 10.32–35, 12.1–11, etc.); but for him the appeal is to Christ as the sufferer and victor, the man who undergoes the harshest temptations and inner struggles in accepting his calling. Christ is the model for the *tempted* Christian: he has gone before into the dark places of doubt and fear and weakness, and endured to death. Our attention is drawn less to the 'finished' reality of Paul's thought, more to the fragmented and uncertain human history behind that reality. The experience of weakness, failure, self-despair of which Paul has so much to say is, in Hebrews, treated less 'programmatically', more pastorally. We are enabled to interpret and so to bear our doubt and pain by the knowledge that our salvation is won by the doubt and pain of Christ. 'Although he was a Son, he learned obedience through what he suffered; and being made perfect he became the source of eternal life to all who obey him' (Heb. 5. 8–9). Our healing lies in obedient acceptance of God's will; but this is no bland resignation. It is a change wrought by anguish, darkness and stripping. If we believe we can experience our healing without deepening our hurt, we have understood nothing of the roots of our faith; Jesus' obedience in the cirumstances of his earthly life, in temptation and fear, 'with loud cries and tears' (5.7), is what opens the long-closed door between God and men's hearts, and, although that door is now decisively open, all must still pass through it to make the reconciliation their own. They must now 'obey' *Christ*, surrender to the pattern of his sacrificial torment and death – not in some kind of constructed self-immolation, but in response to the trials encountered simply in living as a believer, living in the insecurities of faith, 'the conviction of things not seen'. It is an acceptance of the hidden God and his strange work, the God who is only attained through stripping and the purgation of his 'consuming fire' (12.27). We go to him, as did the saints of the old covenant, by going *out*: out of the camp, out of the city (13. 12–14), beyond the settled and the ordered, to the place where Jesus died in his night, his desert.

> The desire to be in God's image without attaining Christ's image is a desire for immediacy, which wants everything without detour and without self-actualization, a narcissistic desire of the ego to settle down in God, immortal and almighty, that doesn't find it necessary 'to let its life be crucified' and to experience the night of pain.

Thus Dorothee Sölle, in her passionate and moving book on *Suffering* (p. 131), reiterates the New Testament's protest against a 'spirituality' without conflict, against the illusion that God is to be found apart from Jesus crucified. But at the same time it is one of the great strengths of her study that she consistently refuses to identify the *acceptance* of pain with passivity in the face of it, a passivity which is, in fact, hardening and dehumanizing. The Christian meets pain in acceptance and *hope*; he or she confronts it, identifies with those experiencing it, and then struggles through it to grow into a new human-ness, 'more capable both of pain and of love' (p. 134). In suffering, the believer's self-protection and isolation are broken: the heart is broken so as to make space for others, for compassion. In this perspective, pain is borne in hope of a new and more compassionate humanity; and here, returning to the New Testament, we may speak again of the Holy Spirit's work. The Spirit is 'pledge', the Spirit is that which more and more conforms to Christ; and so the Spirit is that which impels us forward, which creates hope out of our cries of protest in the present. We protest because we have tasted the reality of new life, God's life, already, the life of self-gift and self-forgetting; so that we know that our present pain is not the whole of reality, that behind it is a more final fact, God's vulnerable love drawing us forward. For God is *in* our pain and our protest: the Spirit, says Paul, is 'bearing witness with our spirit' (Rom. 8.16) to our destiny and our hope, and prays in us 'with sighs too deep for words' (8.26). The crying and longing of the homesick creation is the Spirit's crying. It is in and by the Spirit that we call on God as 'Abba!' in his Gethsemane, at the depth of his fear and doubt. The cry to God as Father in the New Testament is not a calm acknowledgement of a universal truth about God's abstract 'fatherhood', it is the child's cry out of nightmare. It is the cry of outrage, fear, shrinking away, when faced with the horror of the world – yet not simply or exclusively protest, but trust as well. 'Abba, Father, all things are possible to thee' (Mark 14.36). From the middle of the night, we recognize the finality of God's mercy and acceptance. Even when there is no comfort given, there may still be hope: 'not what I will, but what thou wilt' (ibid.). Hope is in trusting whatever God may will; and this is pre-eminently the gift of the Spirit. 'Christ . . . through the eternal Spirit, offered himself without blemish to God' (Heb. 9.14). Our pain is conformed to the pattern of his by the presence of that same Spirit of protest, trust and hope.

The presence of this hope is what makes us alive with 'newness of life' (Rom. 6.4), in the sharing of Christ's *risen* life. Christ's risen life is a life *free* from the threat of death and annihilation ('Christ being raised from the dead will never die again' – Rom. 6.9), the 'threatenedness' that is part of the condition of human sin and distance from God. In sharing this life, we share his freedom from 'threatenedness';

it is never – as is perfectly clear in all Paul's epistles – a freedom from exposure to suffering or from fear, but it is a decisive transition to that new level of existence where *God* is the only ultimate horizon – not death or nothingness. 'From now on, therefore, we regard no one from a human point of view; even though we once regarded Christ from a human point of view, we regard him thus no longer' (2 Cor. 5.16): the 'human point of view', for which death is the final horizon, is put away, and men are free with Christ's freedom. They have, in John's terms, 'passed out of death into life' (John 3.14).

For Paul and John equally, the sign of this passage is a new capacity for love. 'We *know* that we have passed out of death into life, because we love the brethren.' It is a reflection of Jesus' synopsis of the Law and of the parable of the Great Assize (Matt. 25.31–46). It is not that (as some recent writers on the ethics of the New Testament seem to suggest) love is presented as an impossible ideal, to be realized only by grace in the new age; rather the simple assertion that where love is, the Kingdom is, and that reconciliation with the Father is at work, even when unrecognized. The 'un-selfing' involved in union with Christ's death is made real in the public and social world; the displacing of the ego becomes a giving 'place' to others, as God has given 'place' to all in his Son. We love because we are loved (1 John 4.7–11), because our 'place' with the Father is secured by Jesus (John 14.2–3). We know ourselves accepted without qualification, and so have no need of the self-assertive struggle to win a place, a status, a justification. We have understood that the final security is God's gift, and therefore that others will equally find their security in gift – in our humility and 'emptiness' in service to them. 'Love does not insist on its own way,' as Paul has it in his great hymn in 1 Corinthians 13 (v.5); or, in the more comprehensive rendering of the Authorized Version, 'seeketh not her own'. This, as Paul and John agree, is the most clear and enduring mark of Christian identity: not (as, again, it has become fashionable in some quarters to suppose) a benevolence towards all and a generalized wish for their welfare, but an entirely costly *disponibilité*, availability in service which gives no room to the superficial interests of the ego. And it is, once again, something evolving. We have 'put away childish things' in the painful maturity of love, and we move from darkness and enigma in our understanding towards the light of day (1 Cor. 13.11–12). We already have our adoption, our 'place' as children of God, but we cannot begin to imagine the final realization; we know only that it will be seeing God as he is and, in that seeing, being fully conformed to his likeness (1 John 3.2). The end of the believer's life is knowledge of God *in* conformity to God. Knowledge of God is not a subject's conceptual grasp of an object, it is sharing what God is – more boldly, you might say, sharing God's 'experience'. God is known in and by the exercise of crucifying compassion; if we are like him in that, we know him. And we know 'as we are known', 'as I have been fully understood' (1 Cor. 13.12), since God knows the human condition *in* loving it. This knowledge by identification, loving union, is imaged in the appropriating of marital imagery (in 2 Cor. 11.2, Eph. 5 and the final chapters of Revelation) to describe the union of Christ with the believing community, as it had once described God's union with Israel. The Messianic feast at the end of all things is, as in Jesus' parables (Matt. 22.1–10, 25.1–13), a marriage supper; and the longing of the Church and the protesting and struggling Spirit in the Church is the bride's longing for her husband. 'The Spirit and the Bride say, "Come" ' (Rev. 22.17).

Ignatius of Antioch (died *c.* A.D. 110)

It seems more than a little presumptuous to try to reduce the enormous diversity of New Testament models of Christian life to a single pattern; but if it can be done at all, it is because the New Testament churches and their writers existed in virtue of one revealed, lived and acted model: the life, death and vindication of Jesus of Nazareth. Their unity is a unity of direction and vision, not of formulation. Scholars have very properly drawn our attention to the diversity of formulation in the New Testament writings; but that should not reduce us to a negative or agnostic position as to their substantive unity. It is a striking witness to this essential unity of direction in the early Christian communities that we can turn from the New Testament to a set of documents written before the New Testament itself existed as a single collection and find the same pervasive themes. These documents,[1] the letters of Ignatius, bishop of Antioch, provide some of our richest resources for the understanding of Christianity in the immediate 'post-apostolic' period. Written by a man on his way to a degrading and agonizing death, they represent a Christian theology of martyrdom, which is of startling depth and maturity (when one considers that they were written less than a century after the death of Jesus). In the second century as in the twentieth, it is abundantly clear that the theology which emerges from a martyr church will have a very distinctive colouring. In such a situation, it becomes a matter of urgent importance to reflect upon the purposes of God in darkness and suffering and the *engagement* of God in the affliction of his people. Nothing less will be enough to nourish those condemned to die.

Thus Ignatius turns all his polemical vigour against the already vocal school of thought in the Christian world which found it intolerable that the Saviour, the agent and embodiment of God, should share so wholly in the vulnerability of humanity. Ignatius sees both the vastness of paradox here and the inescapable necessity of holding to it in its entirety. God was active to save in Jesus of Nazareth; but this activity extends to the suffering and death of Jesus. Is this suffering (so to speak) purely 'instrumental' to God? or is it *his* suffering? If Jesus wholly and uniquely embodies the merciful agency of God, and remains united to God, faithful to God, even on the cross, that experience, like Jesus' other human experiences, may be said to be taken into God. This is to go a good deal further than St Paul (explicitly) went; but there is evident continuity. The conceptions of a pre-existent 'person' of the Redeemer, making himself 'poor' and exposing himself to pain for our sakes, which are to be found scattered

[1] Throughout this section 'Romans' refers to Ignatius' epistle of that name, not to Paul's, which is designated as 'Rom.'. 'Ephes.' refers to Ignatius' epistle to the Ephesians, 'Eph.' to Paul's.

in the Pauline literature, point the way fairly clearly to Ignatius' bolder language. For Ignatius, Jesus is 'our God' (Romans, Prologue and ch. III): he stands with God the Father over against 'the world', and to desire him is to set aside desire for this world (Romans VI, VII). And so the death of Jesus is 'the passion of my God' (Romans VI), and salvation is born from 'the blood of God' (Ephes. I). Jesus, 'the one true physician', is God in flesh, 'generated and ungenerated'; 'true life in death' (Ephes. VII); and so his death, the death of God, is that which uniquely gives meaning to the death of the martyr.

But there is equally a sense in which the death of the martyr gives meaning to the death of God-in-man. The martyr has no illusion about the reality of his bonds, his fear and his pain; yet in it he knows the closeness of God. 'To be in front of the wild animals is to be in front of God' (Smyrn. IV). Here he is united with Christ's pattern; he is in that same matrix where reconciliation and healing are born out of the meeting between God and suffering. If this is experienced by the martyr, he has a personal assurance of the reality of the Lord's sufferings: they cannot be *less* real than the martyr's, for the martyr looks to Christ's cross as the source of his own capacity to endure. There is a circle of interpretation: the martyr finds God in his suffering because he is assured that his Christian identity as a child of the Father, as a redeemed person, is the fruit of Christ's cross (ibid. I); and the 'content' of Christ's crucifixion, the nature of what was there endured and enacted, is filled out by the present experience of the martyr. All this is contained in those simple words in the letter to the Smyrnaeans: 'If all this was done by our Lord in appearance only, then my chains are also nothing more than appearance' (Smyrn. IV). And a similar process of reasoning seems to lie behind Ignatius' descriptions of his own death as sacrificial, an offering on behalf of the churches. It will be a 'libation' (Romans II), a self-'devoting' (Ephes. VIII, Trall. XIII, Polycarp VI): from the encounter of God with pain and death in Ignatius will flow grace for the churches, because Ignatius is at one with the great encounter and sacrifice in Jesus which is the ultimate well of grace and healing.

Martyrdom, though, is no isolated episode in Christian life.

The oblation begins long before, and the self-devotion, the sacrifice, is both present now and still to be consummated (Trall. XIII). Ignatius' concern with obedience and charity within the Church, even the often-repeated injunction to be in accord with the bishop (Ephes. III–VI, Magn. III, VI, Trall. III, XII, Smyrn. VIII, etc.), is directed towards the education of Christians in sacrifice. The Church is the place where selfless service is learned, in the daily rub of communal life. 'Try to conform yourselves to God's ways by showing reverence to one another' (Magn. VI): God has served and 'reverenced' his creatures, and Christ is the prototype not of the elder but of the *deacon* (ibid.). This is the Christian calling, then: to image in the life of the community the reverence shown by God to humanity in his incarnation, his coming 'not to be served but to serve'. And the pattern of authority in the community must reflect this clearly; the bishop presides according to the *typos*, the pattern, of God. In a letter to Polycarp, bishop of Smyrna, Ignatius explains what this pattern involves. 'Bear all men', he writes, 'as the Lord bears you. Endure everyone in love, as indeed you already do. . . . Speak to each one in the particular manner appropriate to him, as is God's way with us. Carry the weaknesses of all, like a fully trained athlete' (Polycarp I).

Discipleship is the imitation of God's humility, God's service. When Ignatius is kindly treated at Smyrna by Polybius, bishop of Tralles, he writes to the Trallian church that he has experienced the generosity of the whole community in the person of its bishop and is delighted to know through this that they are 'imitators of God' (Trall. I). This service is rendered within the community by such practical acts of charity: the élitist groups already developing in the churches, with their heterodox beliefs, are characterized by a lack of concern for the suffering, the prisoners, the deprived (Smyrn. VI). They do not believe in the truth of Christ's suffering and death, and so they fail in their lives to follow the God-given *typos* of sacrificial compassion. Their Christ is illusory, and in consequence their own lives are phantasmal (Trall. X, Smyrn. II). Faith and love are constantly put side by side in close association (Ephes. IX, XIV, Magn. I, Trall. VIII, etc., etc.). Yet service is not confined to the Christian body: all people have the possibility of turning to God, and the believer must assist them to 'learn about being a disciple' by his actions and his sufferings (Ephes. X). Our service to them is precisely 'proving that we are their brothers' by accepting their anger and hostility without retaliation, being patient with them, and praying unceasingly (ibid.). And in this again we may move towards the *typos* of God's work in Christ, joyfully receiving all insults and injustices (ibid. and Polycarp III).

Thus martyrdom comes as the natural culmination of a far more prosaic process of un-selfing; but it *is* a climax and it is an end to the process and, for Ignatius, a glory and a privilege, the final stamping upon the human coinage of the likeness of God in Christ (Magn. V). And it is also a conformation to the eucharistic self-giving of God; in a startlingly macabre image, he compares his body to grain that must be ground down to make 'pure bread' – ground, in this instance, by the teeth of the beasts in the arena (Romans IV). It seems very likely that this 'pure bread' (and some texts actually add the words 'of Christ' or 'of God') should be seen as parallel to the 'bread of God, which is the flesh of Christ' of ch. VII of Romans; and fragments of eucharistic imagery are scattered in many places throughout the letters. Martyrdom is an 'attaining to' Christ (Romans V), reaching the fore-ordained goal of Christlikeness (it is of interest to compare the use of the verb 'to attain', *epityngchano*, in the New Testament, especially in Rom. 11.7 and Heb. 6.15 and 11.33); and it is growing to mature humanity – 'When I have arrived there, then I shall have become a man' (Romans VI). It seems unlikely that Ignatius should have had in mind any reference to the 'mature manhood' of which Paul writes in Eph. 4.13, 'the measure of the stature of the fulness of Christ': the vocabulary and phraseology are very different (even down to the different Greek words used for 'man'). Yet it would be hard to deny that a similar conception is at work in both passages. Ignatius sees the model of Christ on the cross as that which finally governs human reality: to be human is to be conformed to Jesus crucified; God's purpose for humanity is made clear in the cross. For human beings to 'attain to' the life of God, they must pass through a self-negating death like that of the Lord. And hence comes that most poignant and powerful cry in Romans VI: 'Allow me to be an imitator of the passion of my God! If anyone has God living in him, let him understand what it is I long for, let him share my feelings – for he will know what presses upon me.' It is a 'constraint' like that of Christ himself, longing for the accomplishing of his 'baptism', the kindling of the fire of the Kingdom by his death (Luke 12.49–50). Just as those who question the reality of the Lord's sufferings are themselves unreal, so the martyr has come to *reality*, purity or integrity, authentic humanity. The cross of Jesus and the martyr's identification with it are both revelation and actualization of the truth.

This vivid sense of a unity between truth and life, of a truth present in the flesh of Jesus and the experience of his Church, permeates all the letters; one of its most direct and striking expressions may be found in the letter to the Ephesians (ch. XV). 'It is better', writes Ignatius, 'to keep silence and to be than it is to speak and not to be' (and compare, in ch. VI, the commendation of the bishop's silence). This cryptic remark is explained as he goes on to write about the silence of Jesus. For Jesus, speech and act are one ('He spake and it came to pass'), so that his *acts* are words just as his words are acts; thus, to understand Jesus' words properly *means* to understand his silence, for 'what He has done in silence is worthy of the Father' (ibid.). We may put this passage side by side with Romans VIII, where Christ is referred to as 'the mouth . . . by which the Father spoke'. Evidently (and very importantly) this did not mean for Ignatius that Jesus communicated 'saving truths' from the Father in his teaching, but that he is himself 'what the Father says'. And in both passages, this condition of truthfulness, *being* what the Father says, is presented as the aim of Christian living. Here, then, is another aspect of our conformation to the *typos* of God's work in Jesus, a sharing in that silence of Jesus which is the union of word and deed.

Yet Jesus' silence has still more significance. It is possible to see the whole pattern of his life as the working of God in obscurity and hiddenness, a working 'concealed from the prince of this world' (Ephes. XIX). The conception, birth and death of Christ are 'three mysteries for crying aloud', yet they are 'worked in the silence of God' (ibid.). God spea stuff of material and historical reality, so much so voice is concealed in the 'worldliness' of what he utters it might be said, is Ignatius' version of the Pauline pa. God's election of weakness, obscurity and failure, the folly and weakness of God (1 Cor. 1.17–31). In his letter to the Romans, Ignatius presses this further: 'Our God Jesus Christ is more plainly visible now that He is in the Father' (ch. III). 'Visible' things have no virtue or significance in themselves; and when Ignatius himself has become 'invisible' through his death, he will have attained to true faithfulness to his Lord (ibid.). In that darkness, he will speak more eloquently than ever in his life or his preaching: 'our task has nothing to do with persuasive fluency; for the time when Christian faith is powerful is when it is hated by the world' (ibid).

'My labour pains have begun' (Romans VI). So Ignatius advances to the torture and humiliation of his death in the confidence that there in the arena his true life, his humanity, his *reality*, begin. The truth has appeared in human flesh and suffered human death and thereby created afresh for all humanity the possibility of 'truth' in their flesh and their deaths, of a real and stable ('incorruptible', in Ignatius' language) life constituted by what the world sees as meaningless – silence, failure, death. Truth is not something attained by a stripping-away of the body and the life of the senses in intellectual contemplation. Death is indeed freedom (Romans IV), but never freedom from the body, which is, as for Paul, 'God's temple' (Philad. VII); it is freedom from self and sin, liberation into that service and compassion which God has shown to be his own characteristic activity since Christ is the 'disposition', the 'frame of mind' (*gnome*) of God the Father (Ephes. III). Freedom and truth are already at work in the mutual love and obedience of the Christian gathering; and this is sealed in the sacramental recalling of Christ's self-gift, the Eucharist, which is, in Ignatius' celebrated phrase, 'the medicine of immortality' (Ephes. XX). It is not difficult to accuse Ignatius of morbidity and pathological exaggeration in his attitude towards his coming death; but what makes such an accusation appear shallow and entirely inadequate is the absence in these letters of anything that might be described as self-hatred, and the profound sense in their author that his martyrdom is the climax of his *gift* to the Church of himself. It is here that Ignatius is most deeply united with Paul and with the New Testament in general – in the conviction that fleshly life is not a burden to be borne, nor a prison to be escaped from, but a task to be perfected in grace. It is, indeed (borrowing Eliot's phrase), 'A symbol perfected in death', but only in a death made significant by its relation to the whole of a *life*. So that the life which is marked by service, compassion, poverty, acceptance and so forth is no less intrinsically significant than the death in which it ends, is in fact not separable from it.

At the beginning of Christian spirituality, then, we encounter the conviction that, although Christian life is lived in sharp contradistinction to the life of the 'world' and appeals to a highly specific human experience of encounter with God, it is not founded upon a wholly private or ecstatic experience. To live truly or properly is, in Ignatius' words to the Ephesians (ch. VIII), doing 'fleshly things in a spiritual way': a transformation of the entirety of human experience. It is impossible in the writings of the Fathers as in the New Testament to separate ethics from 'spirituality', and it is an impoverished ethic and a perverted spirituality which sees any kind of competition here between two kinds of claim. One implication of this is that Christian experience and life do not rest upon a past achievement of vision, understanding or knowledge, but are necessarily oriented towards the future, to a goal and a hope. Yet this is – very importantly – not an abstract projection. The 'future' has appeared already: what the Christian life moves towards is the pattern of a human life already *lived*, in the conviction that this life is of enduring authority for all ages because it is the life of God-as-man. And the goal and our struggle are not to be conceived simply as objects of human effort for this very reason, that they are made possible solely by the initiative of God in living out the *typos* of human life – offering himself as a perfected gift and symbol in the world of fleshly life and relations between historical human beings.

The Christianity of the first century is sharply distinguished from other contemporary cults chiefly by this concern with historical reality, and so with growth and conflict in human experience. It pointed to a human life characterized by severe conflict and tragedy as a revelation, not of the hopelessness of the human condition, but of the hope to be uncovered *in* tragedy and of the character of a God who elects for himself the experience of tragic and destructive suffering as a means of self-gift. The 'truth' which the Christian Church preached was more than vision or enlightenment: it was the record of a salvation historically achieved, made available in a concrete community of human beings as a transfiguration of all experience, and the hope and promise of an individual and corporate fulfilment by conformity to the pattern of the redeemer's achievement. Its offer was the offer of life in the Spirit of God's Son and Servant, in communal life and sacramental fellowship – never simply a 'mystery' of cultic participation, but an enduring communion of persons in society. And the oddity of its belief is perhaps made most clear by the attempts of the Church itself to smooth it away; by the sheer embarrassment of so many of its apologists at its particularism and secularity and its implied doctrine of God. The passion of God was to be the boast and the shame of early Christianity. Much of the history of early Christian thought is the record of efforts to domesticate the alien God of Gethsemane and Calvary, the God whom Paul and Ignatius, men very close to the edges of human experience, had so joyfully embraced.

2. The Shadow of the Flesh

The Gnostic Challenge

Letter-writers, by the very nature of their art, are unsystematic and 'occasional' thinkers. Although it is possible to extract coherent patterns from the epistles of Paul and Ignatius, it is only rarely in Paul and never in Ignatius that we find sustained analysis and exposition. Only in the second Christian century does a 'systematic theology' begin to appear, in the writings of such men as Tertullian the African and Irenaeus of Lyons, an expatriate of Asia Minor, who had known Ignatius' beloved Polycarp. And both these writers are prompted to their work by the rapid development of the systems generally called 'gnostic' – a development whose beginnings are clearly witnessed to by the polemic in, especially, the first Letter of John, and elsewhere in the later portions of the New Testament, a polemic directed against those who are denying that 'Jesus Christ has come in the flesh'. Ignatius' opponents who questioned the reality of Jesus' sufferings belong in the same world of thought. But it was the middle of the second century which saw a massive increase in the elaboration of sophisticated gnostic schemes describing the structures of the cosmos and the mechanisms of enlightenment and salvation. It was the most serious intellectual threat that the Church had yet confronted, a complex and subtle religious system, prepared to utilize Christian language in the articulation of a position basically alien to the gospel. The challenge to Christianity was the challenge to define its language, to draw boundaries, above all to defend and justify its commitment to the contingent and the fleshly, to the limits in practice *imposed* on its language by this commitment.

Gnosticism was righly seen by the Christian writers of this period as a flight from the *particular*. Despite the enormous variety of gnostic 'stories' about the cosmos and the soul (stories whose heavy-handed symbolism is unkindly parodied by Irenaeus), there is a clear central motif, summed up by some modern scholars as the doctrine of the 'alien God' and the 'alien soul'. God and the world are strangers to one another: that there is a world is the result of accident or malevolence on the part of some heavenly power. Thus the historical and temporal order, the world of condition and determination, is in no way within the purposes of God; it is an abortion, a calamity. Yet within it, as within all things, are the vestiges of the divine reality in the shape of souls, subjects capable of understanding. And these imprisoned souls must be released to return to their home in God, if they are ever to attain their destiny; thus the religious impetus of gnosticism is the longing to escape from the temporal and the fleshly. There is a single cosmic drama or 'transcendent history' (in Hans Jonas' phrase), in which no significant part can be played by the particular, 'immanent' history of the individual: the pattern of liberation cannot but be the same for all. If this is so, there can be no sense of human experience in its entirety and its individual variety as the theatre of God's saving work, no sense of bodily life as something to be brought to maturity, a work of art to be completed. What is 'authentic' in human life is solely what is radically free from the conditioned and the historical. And the implication to be drawn concerning the life and experience of the redeemer is no less clear: what is significant is the imparting of transcendent, unconditioned truth, pure intellectual communication, the food of the soul, and never the human acts, least of all the human *sufferings*, of a particular man. Hence the gnostic 'gospels', of which a considerable quantity has survived, are records of *words*, not acts, located either at some unspecified point in Jesus' ministry or (very commonly) during the forty days following the Resurrection.

For the gnostic, then, that seriousness about the experiences of conflict and tragedy in the lives alike of Jesus and of his followers which we have seen to mark the earliest Christian spirituality is a sign of spiritual immaturity, a failure to advance into the realm of freedom. There is no problem of reconciliation or integration of experience in gnosticism; although words like 'sin' and 'repentance' may be used, what is in fact being enjoined on the believer is the rejection of certain areas of his experience as illusory and meaningless, irredeemable. Human bondage is not the moral impotence and deadlock of which Paul writes, but ignorance; and not simply ignorance of the state of the self or the motives of action, but ignorance of the 'transcendent history' and of the means for identifying with it – a fleeing from the constraints of human history. 'Jesus, the living one, answered and said: This is the life of my Father, that ye receive your soul from the race of reason, and it cease to be earthly and become wise through that which I say unto you in the course of my words, that ye may complete it and be delivered before the Archon of this aeon and his snares which have no end' (from the 'Books of Jeu'; Hennecke – Schneemelcher, *New Testament Apocrypha*, vol. 1, p. 261). Christ gives to his followers the *information* which they will require in their ascent to God, which will enable them to name and so to overcome the powers which stand in their way. As Harnack long ago observed, gnosticism addresses itself to highly practical questions; the knowledge, the *gnosis*, with which it is concerned is knowledge as power, 'technique', skill in the manipulation of words and ideas in order to find a safe path through the cosmic maze. Rebirth is a 'repossession' of the psyche in the understanding of its true nature as belonging to the family or race, the *genos*, of intellect. It is a part of the basic spiritual reality, *nous*. And the cosmic history is the story of this reality alone, told to men and women in order to provide them with the tools for breaking the prison bars of the pseudo-history in which they live their bodily lives.

Irenaeus of Lyons (*c.* 130–*c.* 200)

The Christian opponents of gnosticism have a good deal to say about this reduction of salvation to spiritual technology. Irenaeus, in his major work *Against the Heresies (Adversus Haereses)*, devotes a long section of the second book to a consideration of the difficult question of God's distinctness from 'nature', *physis*, and therefore from any kind of determined process. The problem, of course, is to state such a distinctness without capitulating to the very view being contradicted. Gnosticism proposes a radical division between an order of bodily nature and an order of spiritual nature: Irenaeus has to set nature, bodily and spiritual, over against the total gratuity of God's dealing with men, and yet avoid a devaluation of this 'nature'. He makes it quite clear (II. 44) that salvation is not 'natural' to the soul, natural in the sense of being potentially within the control of the spiritual side of man, needing only enlightenment to be realized. Salvation is a relationship of love with God, initiated by God's free choice, available to the person living in 'righteousness'. Communion with God is a 'reward' for righteous living (ibid. and I. 2): that is to say, God will give himself to the righteous, but righteousness is not itself simply identical with communion. There is no sort of human activity which *automatically* generates the vision of God, but there are actions which make one 'apt' for the vision of God. And these are, as Irenaeus vehemently insists, the acts of the whole person: 'the things which are proper to righteousness are brought to completion in the body' (II. 44). The life of the soul in itself is nothing. Sense experience, reflection, volition are all matters involving more than the soul (II. 45); soul and body are inseparably bound together, and the soul would have no individuality or identity independently of the body (II. 52–6).

For Irenaeus, then, there *can* be no single 'spiritual' history: God does not have a history, since he does not belong to the order of natural interaction and causality; and man has no history apart from his fleshly existence, in all its contingency and variety. Where the gnostics had pressed God and *nous* together in one spiritual *genos*, Irenaeus forces them apart. He does not deny the unfreedom of the empirical human condition; but unlike the gnostics, he attributes this to the human failure to fulfil the original purposes of God for mankind in history. Man is created in God's image – created with the capacity for relationship to God in obedience: his fulfilment is in this relationship. 'The life of man is the vision of God' (IV. 7). But the image is potential only, it must be made into a 'likeness' by the exercise of goodness (see the *Demonstration of the Apostolic Preaching,* II). Had man been created in perfection, he would have performed his good acts automatically (*Adv. Haer.* IV. 61); and God requires man *freely* to create in his life the pattern of right action. God's will, in fact, is for humanity to make its own history, and within that history to grow towards a sharing in his life. 'The real subsistence of life comes from sharing in God: and this sharing in God means seeing God and enjoying His generosity' (ibid. IV. 34). It is here that humanity has failed, refusing to *grow*, and so condemning itself to imperfect and insubstantial life, subject to 'corruption' – the tendency to disintegration, instability, chaos and, ultimately, death, bodily and spiritual (V. 7). The whole man has been called to realize the likeness of God, and the whole man has failed and is in need of healing.

The only history to be taken seriously is bodily history; and so the redemption of man must be located in bodily history. The gnostics regarded the Old Testament as a grotesque embarrassment, the record of a nation bound to crude and superstitious beliefs about God's involvement with creation. Irenaeus insists upon the *continuity* of God's activity (*Adv. Haer.* IV. 47 ff): the redemptive act is spread over a great length of time in Israel's history, and it is the same God Who is at work in the patriarchs and prophets as in Christ. God makes himself known in vision and 'mystery' to the Jews, and in the words and deeds of the prophets (IV. 34). It is interesting to find Irenaeus drawing attention to the 'prophetic sign', the symbolic acts (and even lives) of such as Isaiah, Jeremiah, Ezekiel and Hosea, as an important means of God's communication to men. Characteristically, attention is being drawn away from words and ideas to the 'speech' of historical fact. In the Old Covenant, God reveals himself under Law and prophecy to enjoin righteousness upon men. By their obedience they may come to true vision of God, and so to share in his life in some degree (IV. 24, 28, 34).

Yet in the Old Covenant there remains a distance between humanity and the God who, although he speaks, remains invisible. If man is to share the life of God, to 'enter into God', God must not only speak but enter humanity (IV. 52); and the prophetic revelation can never go so far. Man, created to be 'the glory of God' (IV. 34), has deprived himself and his world of freedom by Adam's yielding to temptation; he can no longer *create* in his life the icon of God's beauty. So if he is to be restored, no worldly agency can effect his healing, nor can any power outside him. The healing must be enacted in human flesh by the only one who is truly free, the creator himself. Thus the absolute distinction between creator and creation which is fundamental to Irenaeus' anti-gnostic argument is overcome by the divine freedom to act in man's history; but to act in history is to act *as* man, so that the distinction must, at one level, remain absolute. The re-creator can only act as a creature, not as a creator external to the world's history. Thus, in the person of the Redeemer, we know God not 'according to His greatness', *secundum magnitudinem*, but 'according to His love', *secundum dilectionem* (IV. 34). This is not to draw the kind of distinction which later Eastern theologians were to develop between God's 'substance' and his 'operations', but simply to underline the truth that saving knowledge of God is a relationship initiated by God's free decision to love, to delight in, his creation, by his *dilectio*. It is not a vision of majesty or transcendence for us to admire from a distance; it is the encounter with God in the world. We do not *see* the *magnitudo*, and we cannot understand the 'nature' of God. The gnostic error is to assume that such a detached and impersonal knowledge is healing and reconciling, when it is not even possible (ibid. 32). We have seen the incomprehensible Father only in the Son (III. 6 and 11, IV. 11), in a compassion which heals, renews and enlarges our hearts, teaching us that our mortal existence can be transfigured to the likeness of Christ who is the likeness of the unseen Father. 'For when the Word of God was made flesh, He established both these things: He showed us the true image [of God in man] by Himself becoming what was in fact His own image; and He established and restored the likeness [of man to God] by making man resemble the invisible Father by means of [His action as] the visible Word' (V. 16).

This is neatly summed up in a phrase in the *Demonstration of the Apostolic Preaching*, when Irenaeus calls the Son the *gnosis* of the Father (ch. 7): the Father's relationship with the Son is the paradigm of knowledge, the Father knows and is known by the communion he enjoys with the Son. So to know God through or in the Son is to know in communion or 'community of union' (*Demonstration* 6 and 31): it is to possess the Spirit of adoption whereby we have a foretaste of our future relationship with the Father in being enabled to cry 'Abba' (*Adv. Haer.* V. 8, plainly referring to 2 Cor. 1.22 and Gal. 4.6 or Rom. 8.15). We are far away here from the *gnosis* of the Books of Jeu. The goal of Christian growth is a knowledge of God entirely founded in a sharing of life, an intimacy between persons, the fellowship of God with human beings in their humanness. 'In the human race are brought to perfection the mysteries of God which the angels long to see' (*Adv. Haer.* V. 36). Salvation, then, is in no sense a flight to God *from* what is human, but the realizing of God's 'likeness', and so the sharing of his life, *in* what is human. If the world of material and fleshly experience cannot be transformed and saved, the fleshly history of the Word becomes a nonsense (ibid. 14). Again and again we return to this theme of the *visible* Word, the tangible and historical God, the figure in whom life and 'incorruption' are *shown* (*Demonstration* 6, 31, 39); and they are shown in the development and the conflict of an earthly life, a point made abundantly clear in Irenaeus' much-discussed doctrine of 'recapitulation'.

The visible Word is God speaking in the event of Jesus' life and death, and speaking, as always, creatively. The event of Jesus remakes humanity, by its enactment of archetypal human situations in such a way as to direct them Godward. The doctrine of recapitulation (as found in *Adv. Haer.* V. 1 and 10–23, and *Demonstration* 33) is really an extended meditation on Paul's image of Christ as the new Adam; and for Irenaeus this is to be developed with special reference to Adam's temptations. While Adam was tempted and yielded,

Jesus was tempted and endured in obedience. Both are tempted through physical need and instinct (hunger) and through the lure of spiritual power, both are equally vulnerable; but one fails and one triumphs. And thus, it might be said, Jesus creates a new 'archetype' – or, rather, he transforms the Adamic failure into the archetype willed by the creator: the image of God, the possibility of sharing in the divine life, is realized as 'likeness' in Christ's endurance and obedience. 'The human destiny for communion with God', in Wolfhart Pannenberg's phrase, is decisively manifested in this human life in which every significant moral or spiritual option is made an occasion for the development of communion and obedience. And the extremity of Jesus' experience in his passion and descent to Hades further underlines the theme of the sanctification of a *whole* human existence (*Adv. Haer.* II. 22): Jesus has passed through each stage of human development and renewed it – *per omnem venit aetatem* (ibid. III. 19).

As for Ignatius the acts – and the silence – of Jesus constituted the speech of God, so for Irenaeus there is no interest or value in 'saving information' divorced from the human experience of the Saviour. To make salvation a matter of 'saving truths' is to yield the pass to the gnostic, sidestepping entirely the process of healing and integrating the whole of the human person. The saviour whose exclusive task is to pass on information about the spiritual world and its natural laws need have no real historical location: it is wholly appropriate that the gnostic Jesus should communicate his instructions chiefly in the chronological vacuum of the 'forty days' following the resurrection, when he can no longer be supposed to experience any of the constraints of ordinary bodily life. Everything, or almost everything, prior to the resurrection is of limited saving importance; unless, of course, the post-resurrection condition of Jesus' body is projected back into the days of his ministry (as, notably, in the apocryphal Acts of John 88–92, and in the whole docetic tradition with its denial of the reality of Jesus' suffering). In either case, Jesus becomes a figure completely devoid of vulnerability, constraint or conditionedness. And Irenaeus' great theological achievement is to make this very conditionedness, the liability to temptation and the need to choose, central to his view of the economy of salvation. God acts as a creature, and so acts in the full exercise of *creaturely* freedom, freedom practised in response to condition and constraint, so manifesting in the flesh the potentiality of human existence for freedom and stability in communion with God, 'in corruption'. Without the contingent detail of Jesus' earthly life, God does not communicate himself – least of all in discourses about the topography of the spiritual realm. God 'utters' the life of Jesus, he 'speaks' an event, a human history; and so he enters the fabric not merely of human verbal or conceptual exchange but of human society, community, making it the *commixtio et communio Dei et hominis* (*Adv. Haer.* IV. 33), of human language in the fullest sense of the word, a shared 'form of life'.

The consequence of all this for human self-understanding (superbly expounded by Gustaf Wingren in his essay on Irenaeus, *Man and the Incarnation*) is, once again, to draw attention to the experiences of limitation, contingency, temptation and internal and external conflict as fundamental to the mature life of faith and growth towards God. Men and women live between the two poles of 'image' and 'likeness', call and response, opportunity and fulfilment: each human life is, therefore, a continuous story, a *history*, unified by its direction towards the promised communion with God for which it is created. Irenaeus, like Paul and Ignatius in their diverse ways, opens the path to the sense of 'Christian biography', the theological evaluation of how the work of God has united with human variety and contingency in particular lives. The life of Jesus has sanctified the particular, the 'spare and strange', manifesting God in a conditioned human story. Henceforth it is clear that the locus of God's saving action, his will to be known, loved, encountered, is the world of historical decision, whether individual or corporate. It is not and cannot be in a 'privileged', de-historicized ecstasy, nor in the mechanisms of the gnostic's spiritual science. God is encountered as a human person creates his or her life in choosing for or against self-gratifying instinct, for or against power and violence, for or against communion, for or against obedience to the creator. The significant elements of a human life are in these moments of precariousness, of the sense of possibility and freedom. Without the anachronism of simply turning Irenaeus into a second-century Kierkegaard, we may still see in him a thinker for whom creative will is at the heart of human reality, as it is at the heart of God's reality; so that salvation is the encounter and union of these two wills, when human beings will to be what God wills them to be. And Christ, in this system, is pre-eminently the one in whom God's freedom and man's are perfectly expressed.

Alexandria

With Irenaeus, then, 'being like Christ' is being conformed to the pattern shown in an historical life, by means of sharing in the same 'Spirit' mediated through the Church. Other Christian writers, however, were more prepared to take seriously the gnostic's embarrassment about the fleshly Jesus; and for such men, being like Christ must mean being like the Word, the eternal *Logos*, which *dwells* in Christ – conforming not to what is transitory and accidental in Jesus, but to the divine truth veiled in a historical shape. Meditation on the flesh of Christ is important because only by this route do we attain to the eternal Word; but Jesus of Nazareth can never be the terminus of our meditation or our prayer. Here the sharp classical distinction between intelligible form and material or historical embodiment is very evidently at work. The powerful Platonic tradition carried with it an attitude to history which associated historical activity and historical knowledge with the soul's bondage to the material world; and this was to become a pervasive assumption in a great deal of Christian thought. Even (at a much later date) a writer as devotedly concerned with the humanity of Jesus as St Bernard of Clairvaux will unquestioningly repeat that knowledge of or meditation upon the historical Jesus is a mark of the imperfection of an enfleshed spirit whose knowledge cannot yet be pure. The attitude persists: Karl Barth, that least 'gnostic' of modern theologians, still speaks of the 'worldly' form of Christ *veiling* the Word of God, in a way that seems to revive the distinction between a substantial and eternal truth and its accidental and temporal clothing.

The Jewish writer Philo, in the first century of our era, had already attempted to reconcile the uncompromisingly historical revelation of the Old Testament with a non-historical Platonist world-view by reading the sacred texts and the events behind them as an encoded message – as an 'allegory' of eternal truth. His work was to prove of massive significance in the development of Christian reflection on the journey of the soul. For Philo, the goal of the religious quest was a mature *vision*, a *theoria* unclouded by distracting worldly particulars; yet *theoria* was to be learned and practised first on the things of this world. By contemplating the created order, and by contemplating and ordering the moral structure of one's own life, one would be led to the pure *theoria* of the fountainhead of all existence, *ho on*, 'the existing one', 'He Who is', this being the name of God revealed to Moses at the burning bush. Historical revelation in this light becomes God's method of spelling out truth in the terms of the world: an arrangement of clues which, rightly seen, leads to illumination. However, this is not really comparable to the enlightenment of the gnostic: there is no 'technology' here, no suggestion of control over the laws of the Spirit. The end is simply contemplation, the enjoying of God for his sake alone; and Philo shares the biblical repugnance for any suggestion that God can be brought into man's control. God can never be contained in human concepts. Moses ascends into a cloud and darkness beyond the scope of intellect, where God offers himself directly to the vision, without the intervention of any form or idea. Here, then, the pilgrimage of the understanding is seen not (as for the gnostic) in terms of acquisition but in terms of stripping away, the stripping of multiple and diffuse kinds of apprehension to the simplicity of a single-hearted vision – in Platonic terms, the return from the Many to the primal One.

This is the model underlying much of the work of those Christian theologians who lived and worked in Philo's city of Alexandria. They will often make use of terms like *gnosis* and 'gnostic', but it is important to distinguish their views from those of the gnostics rightly so called: like Philo, they retain a strong sense of God's inaccessibility and freedom. Yet they share with both Philo and the gnostics an uneasiness about the fleshly and historical order. Revelation is always conceived primarily as the communicating of saving information; and although it issues in love, *agape*, as well as *gnosis*, the main concern is with the *nous*, the spiritual understanding. Knowledge, a 'grasping' of the mysteries of God, is the beginning of the spiritual life. So Clement of Alexandria (*c.* 150–*c.* 215), the most celebrated exponent of 'Christian *gnosis*', can write in his sermon on *The Rich Man's Salvation (Quis dives salvetur* 7) that God is grasped by *gnosis* and *katalepsis*, 'comprehension', but goes on to explain that this involves *agape* and likeness to God in attitude and life. However, man's likeness to God is explained elsewhere in terms of sharing in God's self-determination and freedom from passions *(apatheia; Stromateis* VIII. 13). Man is in God's image in so far as he possesses *nous*, understanding, and is capable of being *logikos*, of acting, like God, according to *logos (Protreptikos* 78); so when he attains to free self-determination and passionlessness, he is fully capable of rational, *logike*, activity, and so fully in God's image, sharing God's life. He has entered upon the 'divine inheritance' of *aphtharsia*, incorruption, and *atreptos zoe*, unchangeable life (*Quis dives* 27); he enjoys fellowship with God and comes to be more and more 'within' God (ibid.). He is naturally superior to animals in possessing reason, but now comes to surpass them in his Godlike stability as well (*Protreptikos* 93). Even on earth, the 'gnostic' sits 'upon the throne of repose' (homily *To the Newly-Baptized*); he is 'holy and godlike, bearing God in himself and being borne by God' *(Stromateis* VII). By his growth in understanding, he has come to share fully in God's rationality, the eternal *Logos*. The unifying theme in all of Clement's reflections is precisely this, the nature of God and man alike as 'reasonable', the encounter of God and man through the activity of *logos* in both. When Clement quotes Paul on attaining to the Christlike 'perfection of manhood' (Eph. 4.13), he is referring to the 'passionless' condition of the eternal Logos (*Stromateis* VII.10).

The place of Christ in this scheme is essentially that of an instructor. God conforms human beings to his likeness by the *didaskalia* of revelation *(Protreptikos* 71): the Logos teaches the whole universe by giving philosophy to the Greeks and law to the Jews ((*Stromateis* VII.6). And Jesus is the crown of the divine revelation, the 'minstrel' *(Protreptikos* 4), the final manifestation of the divine attractiveness (*Stromateis* VII.10). Clement, in a characteristically fine phrase, says that 'the Lord descended, man ascended' *(Protreptikos* 86), and that 'God has become a fellow-citizen with men' (ibid. 90); but the Ignatian and Irenaean concern with the saving effect of God's sharing human *limitation* is not to the fore. The aspect of limitedness in the earthly life of Christ is clearly ascribed to educational necessity, condescension to the limitations of the created and flesh-bound understanding. Christ spoke simply and directly to his followers because of the weakness of their minds, but the mature believer's task is to penetrate behind the veil of this simplicity to the spiritual kernel. Thus in Clement's long discussion of the story of the rich young ruler, the command to sell all and give to the poor is interpreted as a warning against 'thoughts about riches . . . liking and desire for them' (*Quis dives salvetur* 11). 'Salvation does not have to do with external things and possessions, whether they are many or few . . . but with the virtues of the spirit' (ibid. 18). The spiritual sense of the commandments and the sayings of Christ is concealed from the ordinary believer; but the *gnostikos* knows how to read the Scriptures and interprets revelation aright (*Stromateis* VII.60). At several points, Clement contrasts the 'gnostic's' correct use of Scripture with the crude aberrations of the heretics (ibid., 95, 96, 102, 103). Spiritual maturity is to encounter the eternal, immutable Logos where the uninstructed find only the earthly Jesus. It is noteworthy that Clement's references to the cross are very few; in the *Protreptikos* (91), it is mentioned simply to make a rhetorical point: Christ, bound to the cross, looses men from the bondage of corruption.

Clement unambiguously proposes a sharp distinction between Christians at different levels of understanding. 'Faith' is something which he sees (in a rather post-Enlightenment fashion) as an inferior and uninstructed response to reality; it needs to be 'made perfect by insight' (*Stromateis* VII.55) and supplemented by *gnosis*. *Gnosis* in turn leads to love, and love to the 'heavenly inheritance' of passionless repose (ibid.). Faith is knowledge of the bare essentials, the skeleton, of saving truth, but true *gnosis* is the 'demonstration', the experiential proof, of what is received in faith (ibid. 57). Thus the whole pilgrimage of the soul is presented in terms of knowledge leading to love: the pivotal moment of conversion is the transition from 'uninstructedness' to 'cognition' *(Protreptikos* 75). When a human being realizes his or her true nature of God's child and God's image, that is, when he or she recognizes the rationality of human nature, conversion is effected. 'You are a son . . . so acknowledge the father' (ibid. 79). It is now possible to obey the saving commandments which make man 'worthy of his parentage' *(Stromateis* VII.47), he does not immediately attain to perfection; and his growth will continue on the other side of the grave (ibid. 57) until the full vision of the 'bosom of the Father' is attained (*Quis dives* 36). Clement's is by no means a static model. And, although the 'gnostic' enjoys a spiritual vision superior to that of other believers, this does not exempt him from sharing the worship and life of the community. He cannot be indifferent to others; he will 'consider the grief of others as his own' *(Stromateis* VII.78); he even prays 'to be counted as sharing in the sinfulness of his brothers' so as to stir others to penitence (ibid. 80). Above all, he must share what he has received (ibid. 4, 19, 80, etc.): his conforming of himself to the pattern of God by love and benevolence includes the readiness to instruct and enlighten (ibid. 13). The distinction between the different kinds of believer is certainly not fixed permanently. The gnostic's task is to make more gnostics.

It should be clear that Clement's Christian *gnosis* is distinguishable from the systems of Irenaeus' opponents. The free grace of God, 'the freshness of grace', as he calls it in the *Quis dives* (8), is central to his thought, and he makes a point of commending those classical philosophers who recognized the incomprehensibility of God (*Protreptikos* 59–61) and criticizing the Stoic and debased Aristotelean doctrine that 'the divine' penetrates or animates the material universe (ibid. 58). In other words, he is no less concerned than Irenaeus to insist on God's freedom from any kind of natural order, material or intellectual. Yet Clement, as much as the earlier gnostics, is engaged in a thoroughgoing attempt to 'internalize' the gospel, and it is this which gives his work its pervasive ambivalence. Much (rather too much) has been written about Clement's 'humanism': the sheer beauty of much of his writing, the references to the divine loveliness (as in *Stromateis* VII.10), the insistence that the gnostic should use creaturely pleasures properly and thankfully, in a spirit of detachment (ibid. 62–4, and *Quis dives, passim*). All these have been used to show that Clement's attitude to the creation is affirmative. But Clement is able to write thus about the goods of this world for the simple reason that 'salvation does not have to do with external things': there is no necessary correlation between spiritual state and material condition or action. So, paradoxically, material goods can be enjoyed precisely because they are insignificant. *The Rich Man's Salvation* is a novel exercise in Christian literature; earlier writings from less comfortable churches (notably the Church in Rome in the early second century) had followed the prophetic tradition of stressing in a very literal and unenlightened way the perils of material wealth. Clement, however, succeeds in demonstrating that wealth *need* not be a problem for the believer, provided the transitoriness of every material condition is recognized. He may quote Paul's admonition to the Corinthians to behave, in marriage, in business, in any worldly affairs, 'as if not' (1 Cor. 7.29); but Clement's detachment is not that of someone who believes in an imminent end to all worldly things, which is what Paul takes for granted. The 'gnostic' is in many ways an admirable figure, whose qualities any cultivated man of the period would instantly have recognized; what is absent is any note of stress or difficulty, any acknowledgement of temptation. The biography of Clement's virtuous believer is a smooth path of spiritual advancement.

It would be wrong to accuse Clement of individualism or even of spiritual complacency. But the devaluation of the flesh with its 'fetters' (*Stromateis* VII.40) means that significant history or biography is more or less limited to the private sphere and does not in any very clear sense 'come under judgement' at any point. Indeed, 'judgement' is a concept almost entirely replaced by enlightenment: Christ's presence is illuminating, but seldom so in the Johannine sense of exposing, polarizing, compelling decision. And this is understandable if attention is constantly directed to the teaching rather than the acts, the whole history, of Jesus. Imitating the divine activity is not radical self-oblation, as for Ignatius, nor creative obedience, as for Irenaeus, but the practice of quietude (*hesychia*) and the communication of enlightenment. Certainly this is connected with the gnostic's love of God and compassion for humanity, but it is the compassion of a Bodhisattva – the enlightened man who sacrifices his repose for the sake of enlightening others. The ideal is a serious and important one: what is not clear is how it is to be integrated with a Christian perspective of the Irenaean kind, concerned not with enlightenment but with conversion and transformation. Clement is less of a humanist than many more ascetic or rigorist writers, because his ideal believer *uses* but does not actively *transform* the world; even his dismissive attitude towards places of worship and works of art (*Stromateis* VII.28), with its understandable and praiseworthy scepticism about pagan superstition, reflects something of this. Like Plato, Clement is tempted to banish the artists, whose mingling of truth and falsehood in the medium of worldly stuff, words and things alike, is the most powerful delusion threatening the soul. For truth is not to be found intertwined with contingency; it is always a homeless stranger in the historical order.

Origen (*c.* 185–254/5)

Turning to the greatest representative of Alexandrian Christianity, Origen, we find a far more subtle and differentiated scheme, yet one that labours under many of the same difficulties as Clement's. It has been well said of Origen that in him the 'disciple of Jesus' coexists very uneasily with the Platonic speculative philosopher. If Clement's progression is from faith to knowledge and from knowledge to love, Origen is far less inclined to make a clear division between these stages: for him, knowledge and love go hand in hand. 'Whenever we enquire in our hearts about divine teachings and their interpretation, and discover the truth without the help of teachers, then we may believe that we are being kissed by our bridegroom, the Word of God' (*in Cant.* I 331.1).[1] 'Our bridegroom, the Word of God': there is the heart of Origen's thinking. We do not even begin to pray unless we are first touched by 'the inner wound of love', which impels us to seek ever more direct and personal experience of Christ, comparable to the relation of married love; once touched by our lover, we can no longer be content with what is mediated of his love in the Church, through 'angels and prophets', but desire to transcend even the freedom and rationality proper to mankind and receive the direct supernatural enlightenment of the Word (ibid. 329). Origen gives voice to the longing which has never been quenched in any religious tradition, the passion, not for 'intellectual' ecstasy or even for a mystical absorption, but for direct, palpable assurance and experience of the *sweetness* of a God who enters into intimacy with his creatures. Certainly, even in the great *Commentary on the Song of Songs*, the delight and sweetness is conceived in highly intellectual terms; yet for Origen the discernment of truth, the resolution of difficulties, the grasping of *meaning* is a personal and relational matter. To know only at second hand, in teachings and stories, fails to provide 'the full and perfect satisfaction for the soul's desire and love' (ibid. 330). Intellect and heart are not separable, love and understanding are unthinkable in isolation from one another.

Origen's concern with direct experience may give a rather individualistic colouring to his thought. Yet the whole of the *Commentary on the Song of Songs* moves back and forth between the corporate and the individual, the Church and the soul, and there is never any pretence that the experience of the particular soul is independent of that of the Church as a whole (a good example of this alternation can be found in iii. 39–41); and the enlightening of the soul is designed to issue in the building-up of the Church' (iii. 61). Again, in Origen's treatise *On Prayer* (XI, 1 and 2), we read that the prayer of Christ the high priest unites with all the prayers of

References to this work are according to the Lommatzsch pagination in Baehrens' 1925 Leipzig edition men and of angels; and that the departed saints, now made more perfect in love, are better able to pray with and for the Church on earth, bearing the griefs and burdens of those still struggling in their pilgrimage. Origen never loses sight of the vision of the Church as a community *sharing* experience, imitating its Lord by identification with the suffering. In a homily on Leviticus (X.2) he writes that fasting for the sake of helping the poor is 'truly acceptable to God . . . because it imitates Him Who laid down His life for His brothers'. 'Christ counts the sufferings of the faithful, and everything that befalls them, as His own' (*de oratione* XI.2), and that is the model for Christian prayer as for Christian behaviour in general. Thus Origen as much as Ignatius or Paul is concerned to present the Christian life as an imitation of the *incarnate* Lord, who identifies himself with and offers himself for an imprisoned and suffering humanity. Christian growth is growth towards the pattern of kenotic compassion, begun on earth, perfected hereafter (*de orat.*XI.2); and 'the adornment, the necklace, placed upon the "neck" of the Church is the obedience of Christ' (*in Cant.* ii.416). When the Church's humility grows to the measure of Christ's, the Church has its finest adornment. And in the *Exhortation to Martyrdom*, Origen (writing here in his old age, in the face of a persecution under which he was to suffer greatly) follows Ignatius in envisaging Christian maturity in terms of the martyr's death. In baptism we have committed ourselves to the way of the cross: martyrdom is the final test of the reality of self-denial (XII). Readiness for martyrdom is a 'yielding place to the Spirit', who comes to be fully present when reviling and humiliation are the believer's lot (XXXIX). Unless the sufferings of Christ 'overflow' into our lives, his joy and consolation will not 'overflow' in us either (XLII). To accept the cross and confess Christ internally is not enough: 'it could even be said that it is better to honour God "with the lips" when one's heart is far from Him than to honour Him "in the heart" while failing to confess Him "unto salvation" with the mouth' (V; referring to Rom. 10.10 and Isa. 29.13) – a sharp contrast to the attitude of those gnostics who, we are told, excused their apostasy in time of persecution by appealing to the insignificance of external acts and events. Yet the central tension in Origen's thinking is perhaps nowhere more evident than in this treatise, where he appeals in turn to the transitoriness of earthly things and the paramount value of the spiritual order on the one hand, and the following of the incarnate Christ for the sake of the brethren on the other, as incentives to courage in face of martyrdom. The spiritual man should be happy to lay aside the body, regarding death as deliverance from bondage (III); yet the body is the means whereby the likeness of Christ in the world is formed. Origen's treatment of Gethsemane (XXIX) is patently embarrassed, since he cannot conceive of the perfectly spiritual man experiencing fear of death. Far more sensitive than Clement to the centrality of the incarnational model, Origen is still unwilling to abandon the valuation of the spiritual world dictated by his general philosophical view, and the consequent model of salvation as deliverance from the bondage of the material.

It is axiomatic for Origen that the *nous* (spirit, soul, subject, intellect) is 'akin' to God, and so by nature tends Godward (*Exh. Mart.* XLVII). The *nous* is the image of God, created before the body (*Dialogue with Heraclides* 154 ff, *Hom. in Jer.* II.1, etc.), and it alone can know God (*contra Celsum* VIII.38,39). Thus the knowledge of God is very sharply distinguished from sense-experience of any kind (*contra Celsum* I.19, VII.33–46 *passim, Hom.* 27 *in Num.*, etc.). The material world, as for the gnostics and Origen's Platonizing contemporaries, represents a falling-away from unitary spiritual reality, and God cannot therefore be known under its forms. And furthermore, Origen inherits from both Plato and Philo the conviction which we have already noted in Irenaeus and Clement that God is, in himself, radically unknowable, that he cannot be circumscribed under any concept and does not 'participate in being' (*contra Celsum* VI.64). He is not a thing and belongs to no class. Human nature cannot attain to the wisdom underlying all creation (*de. orat.* I.1), and so the knowledge of God is always a mystery of immeasurable grace. The vision of God as he is would simply annihilate man; so God deals with human beings as they are, as fleshly creatures, hiding himself from 'those who cannot bear the dazzling brightness of knowing Him' (*contra Celsum* VI.17). Thus in our present Christian experience we are in 'shadow'. Commenting on the 'shade' of Song of Solomon 2.3, Origen develops a very complex interpretation of Christ's 'shadow' in which the Church now lives (*in Cant.* iii): as the Law was a 'shadow of good things to come' (Heb.10.1), so Christ casts the shadow of still greater things. The eternal Way, Truth, and Life which Christ is are apprehended in this life by living in Christ's shadow; only by remaining there can we be assured of vision face to face in the age to come. The soul is, in any case, in shadow in this life because it is 'covered' by the body. The overall sense of this richly allusive passage seems to be that, since knowledge in this life is necessarily of shadows and images only, God's grace has set in the world of shadows the shadow of his own truth, so that human beings may know him, even if only indirectly, in this 'mirror and enigma' which is Christ. Origen returns to the same theme in the *Dialogue with Heraclides* (172 ff; compare *de principiis* II.6): we are in shadow because Christ now stands before our eyes; and since he casts the shadow, he has not yet fully appeared to and *with* us (Origen refers to Col.3.3–4). When he does appear as he is, when we see him face to face, we shall be fully united 'with the God of the whole cosmos and His only-begotten Son'.

There is yet more in the *Commentary on the Song of Songs* about Christ as the shadow protecting us from the blazing heat of the devil's assaults; but it is the picture of Christ as the shadow of divine truth which is of most interest in the overall assessment of Origen's spirituality. To know Christ is the highest privilege of man as a fleshly being; but man is not only, and not ultimately, fleshly. Therefore Christian maturity will involve a progressive detachment from the fleshly Jesus. Our initial simple commitment to Christ crucified must give way to the 'interior gospel' (*in Joann.*I.7–8). This progression is treated in detail in the twenty-seventh *Homily on Numbers,* where faith in the incarnation is seen as the first stage of our deliverance, the first step in the struggle against the purely natural life, with its passions and illusions. The ascent is towards total detachment from fleshly nature and its manner of knowing. The same theme is evident in Origen's celebrated distinction begween 'moral,' 'natural' and 'contemplative,' (*inspectiva*) knowledge, in the Prologue to the *Commentary* *on the Song of Songs* (307–313) – contemplative knowledge being that supra-sensible knowing to which a proper exercise of the inferior methods leads us. Thus knowing Christ after the flesh is bound to be, for the spiritual man, a preparation for the final true knowledge of the eternal Word, the Word prior to and independent of the incarnation (*contra Celsum* VI.68).

This does not mean that Origen thought Christ a dispensable aspect of Christian belief. The first chapter of the *de oratione* explains that the unapproachable God has made himself our 'friend' by drawing near to us in Jesus. Without Jesus we should have no knowledge of God (*contra Celsum* VI.66, etc.), and all prayer is made through and in him (ibid. V.4, VIII. 13,26,75,etc.; *de orat.* XV, *passim*), and it is (as for Paul) Jesus' relationship with the Father that is determinative for every Christian who has received in baptism the 'spirit of adoption' (*de orat.* XXII.2–3). The Christian destiny is 'to become god in Jesus' (*in Luc. hom.* XXIX): as the Word is the eternal image of God, we, by his indwelling us, become images also (*de orat.* XXII.4), sharing a single activity with the Word (*in Joann.*I.16), the activity which is simply the performance of the Father's will (*de orat.* XXVI.3). And both here and hereafter, the Christian shares in the priestly prayer of the Word to the Father, his constant compassionate intercession for all (*de orat.* X.2). We have already noted Origen's concern with the imitation of the incarnate Lord; here we see how he envisaged the final human destiny as sharing in the activity of the eternal and pre-incarnate Word. Yet there is no sharp division in kind between the action of the Word in eternity and his action as incarnate: both are the actions of sacrificial love and obedience. Origen's Logos is not simply a principle mediating knowledge of God to an inferior reality, but very truly the lover and bridegroom of the soul, bringing human beings to stand where he stands before the Father, uniting the soul to himself as in a marriage (*in Cant. passim, contra Celsum* VI.20, etc.). 'The principal function of knowledge is to "recognize" (*agnoscere*) the Trinity' (*in Cant.* ii. 404): the soul, considering its true nature, will come to certain conclusions about its own destiny, and so will be open to the leading of the Holy Spirit, whereby it receives the grace to know the Father as does the Son. It will 'recognize' or 'acknowledge' the Trinity, presumably, in recognizing that its true nature is to be with the Logos. Origen strongly discouraged the addressing of prayers *to* the Logos (*de orat.* XV.1–4, XVI.1; see also Eusebius' *Praeparatio Evangelica* XIV.6, on Origen's attitude and practice), for the simple reason that the Son prayed on earth and prays in heaven to the Father; if we are with or in the Son, we must do likewise. Origen had no desire to belittle the Son, but for him prayer was essentially an entry into an eternal relationship between Father and Son, in which the Son reflected, obeyed, glorified, loved and prayed to the Father. To worship the Son was pardonable for the ignorant, but the mature should realize that it is in fact a distortion of what prayer most profoundly is – an abstracting of it from its proper context in the life of God himself, where it is 'a glorifying of God through Christ Who is glorified with Him' (*de orat.* XXXIII.1).

How is one to assess a thinker of Origen's range and depth? Many who have written about him have felt the tension noted earlier between the biblical theologian and the speculator, and detailed examination of his work does little to resolve the problem. Yet if the tension never becomes insupportable it is because of the central significance of Origen's clear vision of the divine self-gift in all that he writes. The Logos concept had tended to be for other writers, Christian and non-Christian, a solution to the problem of knowledge and 'participation' – how does the world share in God's being, how is its reality related to the single authentic reality? But Origen's Logos is emphatically the Word made flesh in Jesus of Nazareth, and the reciprocal love of Father and Son gives life to the abstract relation between the Creator and his principle of rationality. Jesus' relation to his Father in love and prayerful obedience tells us more about the eternal Word than any amount of cosmological speculation. In this respect, Origen is always an incarnational and biblical theologian.

Yet there remains, obstinately, the problem of his attitudes to the material world and historical reality. While he never claims that the historical life of man is insignificant, there is no doubt that he sees it as an imperfection and distortion of the truly human. It is fruitless to attempt to deny or even mitigate his Hellenic inheritance, and we must recognize how much this affects his conception of human and Christian growth. What is positive and important in all this, however, must also be recognized. The whole notion of the soul's ascent, from the visible to the invisible, states in Platonic terms a theme which we have already seen to be deeply rooted in Christian reflection: that is, that Christian experience of God is 'oblique' and puzzling. The Christian, who locates the work of his God as *hidden* in a set of particular historical occurrences, can never simply appeal to a private and direct vision of the transcendent. For Origen as much as anyone, God is to be encountered in the world; and although the form in which he is encountered is a 'shadow', yet it is a shadow whose shape is more than merely transient or accidental. In gnosticism, the 'shape' of the Redeemer's life is immaterial to the imparting of saving knowledge; but Origen is committed (sometimes, one must say, in spite of himself) to believing that what we know of Jesus 'after the flesh', and indeed the whole pattern of historical and scriptural revelation is a true image of the nature of the eternal Word. History and Scripture and the incarnate life may be transitory, but they are not accidental. And so it will continue to matter how the Christian behaves 'in the flesh', for he can there form his image of the incarnate image of God, freeing his soul from the bondage of lovelessness, from an acquisitive clinging to what he can control in the world of matter and sense-knowledge. He will be prepared (as Origen describes it in the *Homily on Numbers*) to go into a desert, to go out from what is secure and familiar, like Abraham (*Exhortation to Martyrdom* V), to 'die' into a new and strange world, in which we must 'go forward, never stopping' (*de orat.*XXV.2). It is one of the commonest of errors to suppose that Platonism of any sort simply devalues the finite; after all, if you believe material things to be images of heavenly reality, you will not despise them. The weakness of Platonism, however, is its lack of historical concern: its world is essentially static. Origen succeeds in giving history, story, a place in such a system, and does so not simply by treating the story as a long cipher, as allegory, but by granting that – at least – the history of Jesus is an irruption of grace into the historical world, an historical picture of the eternal

Godhead. That is, it is not illustrative ot a system (as in Philo's exegesis the story of Moses might be held to be), but constitutive of *new* belief and new relationship with God. Where the life of Jesus is concerned, we have to do not so much with allegory (though of course Origen makes extensive use of it in his works on the Gospels) as with the revelation of the God-given ordering of existence – detachment, compassion, the cross, pilgrimage into a strange world of vision and liberty, adoption into sonship. Jesus is not merely a figure representing the new life; as Origen repeatedly insists, he is its source.

The question still remains whether, in spite of all, Origen's view of the incarnation is too 'instrumentalist' to be really acceptable, too concerned with the incarnate life as a means to some superior end. He cannot but see the incarnation as a concession to human imperfection, and he is very reluctant, as we have already noted, to say anything positive about temptation or conflict, in Jesus' experience. There is a sense in which his Christ is less than fully incarnate. This is clear not only in the notorious passages (*in Matt.hom.* C, *contra Celsum* II. 63–6) where he toys with the idea that Jesus could assume different physical forms at will, but in a general unconcern with the human will and human development of Jesus – a sharp contrast with Irenaeus. The story of Jesus remains an external presentation, and all that can be known of Jesus' inner life is his unbroken filial relation with God. And so we come to the paradoxical conclusion that Origen, for whom the external is so often entirely subordinated to the internal, fails at this point to give sufficient weight to the internal. Christ, it seems, has no human 'inner life': Origen allows that in theory Christ had the power of free choice, but claims that in fact 'all possibility of change was removed from [his soul]', (*de principiis* II.6.6). Comparable views were to become more and more common in the early Church, and it is superfluous to point out their results for a doctrine of the humanity of Jesus.

Irenaeus understood the Christian task as the following of Jesus in creating in the world, by the exercise of grace-assisted freedom, a life glorifying God. Clement withdraws the creative will almost entirely into an internal and spiritual sphere.

Origen is concerned about the glorifying of God in the world, and yet is unwilling to see this as emerging, in Jesus or in ourselves, from trial or moral struggle. Temptations are permitted so that we may see more clearly what we *already* are (*de orat.* XXIX. 17–18); they have no very positive or constructive role. The passionless condition of the spiritual man makes him invulnerable on this level. This is perhaps the most important area in which Hellenizing preconceptions have closed certain options to Origen. He is anything but a gnostic; yet there is the same unwillingness, in the long run, to confront the contingencies of the human situation. The preoccupation with the illusory and precarious nature of the material clouds the perception of the precariousness of spirit and will and so, again, leads to an emphasis on ignorance or distance rather than bondage and sin. There are darker shadows than those of the flesh.

3. End Without End

The Arian Crisis

It is not surprising that a writer of Origen's complexity should father so diverse a theological family. In the next two generations of the Church's history there are the most serious theological and spiritual divisions early Christianity had yet known; and both parties in the dispute could reasonably claim to be disciples of Origen. When the Alexandrian presbyter Arius, at the beginning of the fourth century, argued that the Word could not be co-eternal with the Father because the Word, by definition, had a source and the Father had not, he was (as recent scholarship has made clearer than ever) giving logical expression to what seemed to be implicit in a great deal of earlier devotion and reflection – not least in the work of Origen. Origen had, after all, emphasized repeatedly the role of the Word as imaging and responding to the Father; and an image must surely be a secondary and derivative reality. But there is in God no derivation, his proper definition is to be 'without a source' (*agenetos*). And Arius, who had been trained as a logician, probably in the schools of Antioch, drew the conclusion that the Word could not be God: 'there was a time when He (the Word) did not exist', he could be no more than the first and highest of creatures. Thus two aspects of Origen's thought, the absolute transcendence and incomprehensibility of God, and the role of the Word as image and mediator, are brought together as terms in a syllogism. And the argument is further undergirded by appeal to the facts of the Word's incarnate life, those very facts which Origen had found difficult: the Word feels grief, weariness, hunger, fear and pain, and the passionless God can experience none of these things.

What was lacking in this brisk reduction was Origen's vision of salvation as an entry into the divine life, the divine society, 'becoming *theos* in Jesus'. Origen might have been hard put to it to explain how his view of the Trinity differed *logically* from the Arian picture, yet his vision of the eternal loving relation between Father and Son cannot readily be compressed into Arius' scheme, in which the unique status of the Logos was simply a matter of divine grace and election (see, e.g., Athanasius, *contra Arianos* I.35-50). Arius' God is not naturally or necessarily the Father of the Son; Origen's God eternally wills to share his being with 'another', the Word (*de principiis* I.2, IV.28), and through this Word to share himself with creation. Arius was, in fact, proposing a very important revision not of the 'doctrine of the Incarnation' (which could hardly be held to exist at this date) but of the Christian understanding of God. Despite all the philosophical tendencies at work in some earlier writing, the conviction had remained that God and Christ were to be held together, and that the work of Christ was in some sense the work of God. This could not be said of Arianism: the Arian God cannot be directly involved at all in the work of salvation. Thus Athanasius, in his controversial works against the Arians, will repeatedly put the question of how the Arian Logos can save, how he can truly reconcile creation with God when he is himself a creature (see especially *contra Arianos* II.22, 26, 67–70). The Arians, it seems, held that, since God could release men from sin simply by *fiat*, it was immaterial whether or not the Son were a creature. Athanasius, in replying to this (*contra Arianos* II.68), offers a very interesting restatement of the Irenaean position: of course God *can* save by word alone, but this is not 'expedient' for humanity, and what matters is the latter, not the abstract possibilities open to God. Salvation by word alone remains no more than an external assurance: grace does not become internal to human existence, and human history becomes a dreary succession of sins and absolutions. The human world is not *transformed*, grace is not 'joined to the body'. The Son has not only to live a human life, but to die a human death, since without this, death would remain an area untouched and untransfigured by God, and we should never become inheritors of immortality and incorruption (ibid. 69).

Athanasius' argument against the Arians is sometimes reduced to the well-known point that, if salvation is a partaking of divinity (*theosis,* 'deification'), the Word cannot deify if he is not God (see, for example, *de synod.* 51); and it has been said by some that a theology for which 'deification' is no longer important will find this superfluous (the point is well made in Professor Maurice Wiles' article 'In Defence of Arius', now reprinted in his *Working Papers in Doctrine*, pp. 28–37). But it is of first importance to bear in mind that 'deification', for Origen, Athanasius and their successors, did not mean a sharing in the divine 'substance', a quasi-physical participation, but enjoying the divine *relation* of Son to Father, sharing the divine life. In this sense, it could be argued that any Christian theology worth the name will need a doctrine of 'deification' and it is hard to see how Athanasius' point can be put by. Unless the relation of Father and Son is something eternally holding true of God, the relation of sonship to God cannot be realized. Such is the essence of Athanasius' argument, and it makes a serious contribution to the clarifying of the Christian doctrine of God. It would, he writes (*contra Arianos* IV.22), be absurd to suggest that God is our father if he is not first the Father of the Son.

But most significantly of all, Athanasius' case depends upon the capacity of God to involve himself in the historical order. Although he often writes as if the weakness of the incarnate Word were something resulting only from his bodily nature, he allows that ignorance, sorrow and fear are no less a part of his earthly condition (*contra Arianos* III.34). 'Flesh', for Athanasius, evidently means the whole order of contingent worldly existence. Awkwardness remains, notably in the notion (to become a commonplace in both Eastern and Western Fathers) that the activities of divinity and humanity are discernible, so to speak, side by side in the life of Jesus: 'In the case of Lazarus, He spoke as man, in a human voice, but raised him from the dead in a divine way, acting as God' (ibid. 32). In this naive distinction, we are some way from the Irenaean Christ, whose divinity is manifest in his fulfilled and perfected humanity. Nonetheless, Athanasius unambiguously affirms that we cannot deny in advance God's ability to be incarnate on the grounds of a preconceived notion of the divine transcendence; nor can we deny God's ability to be Father and Son on the grounds of a preconceived definition of the divine simplicity. The constructs with which the unknowable and unique nature of God had been explained and defended turn out in practice to be constraints upon the divine freedom: so far from protecting the transcendence of God, they limit him to words and concepts. The Athanasian God 'transcends His transcendence' to be encountered in human shape: his hiddenness and unknowability are grasped in and through the weakness of the flesh of Christ. We return again to the theme of the *oblique* character of Christian knowledge of God, discerning God as hidden in what is not God, knowing him as the One who does not let himself be known, and so forth. We do not begin from innate or intuitive ideas of the absolute or the transcendent; we are drawn into a transformed life, speech and activity in which the inexhaustible resource of the God who draws us is gradually discovered. And the agent of that 'drawing' is the historical figure of Jesus, through the relations with himself which he establishes in Church and Sacrament. The believer learns to know God in Christ in the enduring of suffering and temptation because in all such situations he will discover the God who is not destroyed or exhausted by them; he continues to call into a future. Whether or not Athanasius wrote the *Life of St Antony* ascribed to him, he was unquestionably closely connected with the early monastic circles there described; and (as we shall see in a later chapter) the early monks were profoundly concerned with the necessary and positive role of temptations. Certainly they conceived their vocation as the creation of God-reflecting communal life. And we read in the *Life* (44) that Antony's disciples not only strove to live in 'love and harmony', but were characterized by their 'hope for the future'. It is here that we must look for 'Athanasian' spirituality.

As the fourth century advanced, the outlines of the debate

became increasingly clear. The 'left wing' of the Arian party pressed for a recognition of the radical *un*likeness between Father and Son, and their most articulate representative, Eunomius, pushed Arian transcendentalism to its most extreme expression, in the curious doctrine that only one name could be truly predicted of God, the name *agennetos,* 'unborn' (*not* simply *agenetos,* 'without a source'), and that this was literally all that could be known of God even by himself. According to his opponents, Eunomius vehemently denied that *agennetos* was merely one possible conceptual counter among others in talking of God (Gregory of Nyssa, *contra Eunomium* II.42,44 – 'he says that "unborn" should not be predicated of God only notionally'); and a section of his own apology (in Migne, PG 30, 842D) suggests the same. Thus the response to Eunomius concentrates upon the inadequation of our concepts and words to the reality being spoken of. Knowledge of God cannot stop at a definition, a label; indeed, Eunomius' opponents go on to say, knowledge of *anything at all* is something which goes beyond definitions, because it finds itself incapable of halting and summing up its investigations (Gregory of Nyssa, ibid. II. 67–78, III.viii.1–4). And this is most true of our knowledge of ourselves, of the mystery which, for convenience, we call 'soul', even though it is impossible to say what we mean by such a term (ibid.II.106–118). Words and names change, necessarily, as our relations to things or persons develop. Changes in language may not alter the nature of an object, but the function of speech is nonetheless to articulate a changing relation as 'the understanding makes contact with things' (ibid. III.v.52). Nor, in speaking of God, can we avoid analogies from the material and human world (ibid.48–9). There can be no 'privileged' concept of God with assured priority over the language produced by Christian life and common experience. The one truth of which we *can* be sure is that God escapes all definition in his freedom; and if we come to know God in the flesh and in the sufferings of Christ, we are not to conclude from this that God is naturally vulnerable, but should wonder at the power of God to *make* himself weak and identify himself with a life not his own (ibid.III.30–40).

His limitation in Christ becomes a sign of his sovereign freedom from all limitation, from the tyranny of concepts.

The Cappadocian Fathers

Basil of Caesarea (*c.*330–79) and his brother Gregory of Nyssa (*c.*330–95), the authors of the major replies to Eunomius, were both deeply involved with the monastic movement, and in their work we may see again the close connection between theological positions and forms of Christian life. Of Basil's monastic 'rules' we shall have more to say in a later chapter. But it is worth noting that Basil's strongly practical and communitarian vision of the ascetical life is bound to his conviction that the knowledge of God is found only through the practice of self-crucifying service, in imitation of Christ. The monk's 'philosophy' is the pattern of the incarnate Christ. It is Gregory, however, who elaborates more systematically a theology of the Christian spiritual life, a theology deeply marked by Origen's concern with the union of love and knowledge and with the goal of the Christian life as an entry into the trinitarian relationship. But perhaps his most important contribution to Christian thought was (and is) his sophisticated development of Origen's view of Christian life as unceasing advance, 'straining forward to what lies ahead' (Phil. 3.13, quoted by Origen in *de orat.* XXV.2). As two recent German writers on Gregory (E. Mühlenberg and Josef Hochstaffl) have emphasized, he sees 'negative theology' in a positive light, as the ground of man's self-transcendence: 'From the insight that the knowledge of God can never reach a terminus, Gregory of Nyssa developed the idea of an unending self-transcendence of human beings in their relation with God' (Hochstaffl, *Negative Theologie,* p. 109). And the late Cardinal Daniélou, probably the greatest interpreter of Gregory in this century, placed at the heart of his study, *Platonisme et théologie mystique,* the concept of *epektasis,* 'straining forward', the noun deriving from the verb used by Paul in Phil. 3.13. Gregory himself, at the beginning of his treatise *On the Life of Moses (de vita Moysis)* writes, 'One definition [*horos*] of the perfection of the virtuous life that we are taught by the apostle is that it has no limit [*horos* again],' (300 D).

On such a foundation, the Hellenistic doctrine of the 'kinship' between the soul and God, argued by Clement and Origen alike, becomes insupportable. If there can never be real intellectual unity between the soul and God, if the soul's knowledge of God is always characterized by a measure of 'bad fit', the relation between the two is always a relation between *distinct* realities, a greater and a smaller. Gregory leaves no room for any 'absorption mysticism'. He will faithfully repeat, in many works, the commonly accepted view of the soul as 'nobler' or 'higher' than the body and, like Origen, believes that the soul is the proper image of God, created before the body, which is only 'the reflection of a reflection' (see *On the Making of Man* [*de hom. op.*] XII, PG. 44, 161D – 164A); but in his ascetical and ethical thinking, there can be no doubt that the dignity of the soul as intellectual subject occupies a relatively minor place as a theme. In his commentary on the Beatitudes, he says simply that, since 'intellectual' knowledge of God is impossible, he must be found and known in the converted heart of the believer and in the purity of his or her life and actions (*de beat.* VI, PG.44, 1268 – 1272C). 'The understanding is incapable of attaining to him who truly exists' (ibid. I. 1197B). Thus the focus of attention is subtly shifted from the experiences of the interior life to the whole history of human growth; more than most previous Christian writers, Gregory exploits the classical term *arete*, 'moral virtue', in this writing, regarding the attainment of this quality as the end of all 'spiritual' experience. And *arete* is itself purged of its traditional Hellenic associations of aristocratic dignity and self-approbation by being envisaged as essentially the service of God and men, after the pattern of Christ.

The concept of participation in the divine was, as we have already seen, a very important part of the religio-cultural world view in which the early Church generally shared. Gregory determinedly revises the notion so as to direct attention to participation not in what God is, but in what he *does*. 'The man who shares with the poor will have his share in the One Who become poor for our sake' (*de beat.* I. 1208 B). 'Human beings must become what they copy' (*On the Lord's Prayer, de orat. dom.* V. PG.44 1180 B–D): we, like God, are free (and freedom is one of the most important aspects of the image of God in man for Gregory), and free, therefore, to forgive as he forgives (ibid. 1180 A). We must so imitate the divine pity that we may have the boldness to say to God, 'Copy your servant, Lord, Your poor and needy servant. I have forgiven, now You forgive' (ibid. 1180 CD). To become God, then, is to act as God acts, in love, in poverty, in compassion. There is no hint here of any internalizing of the gospel's requirements: commenting both on 'Give us this day our daily bread' and on 'Blessed are the poor in spirit', Gregory has harsh words for the wealthy, whose daily bread is eaten at the expense of others. And his interpretation of the command to sell all and give to the poor (*de beat.* I. 1208 A) is literal enough to dismay the shade of Clement. Nowhere is Gregory closer to the spirit of his brother, whose monastic communities were intended to be centres of practical charity for the poor and sick and disadvantaged. It may be an exaggeration to say that 'the monastic movement was in a real sense an effort after social righteousness' (E. F. Morison, *St Basil and His Rule,* p. 7), as if this alone were the primary impetus behind the monastic movement; yet there is no doubt that Gregory and Basil considered 'social righteousness' inseparable from the vocation to participate in the divine life. 'Deification' includes washing the feet of the poor.

This may throw a little light on the vexed question of Gregory's (and Basil's) occasional references to the believer's participation in the 'power' or 'energy' (*dynamis* or *energeia*) of God, rather than in his substance (*ousia*). This was later to become one of the bases for the medieval Greek theory, associated with the name of St Gregory Palamas, the fourteenth century archbishop of Thessalonika, that God subsisted in three modes, 'persons', 'substance' and 'acts' (*energeiai*): to know God is to know and participate in his 'acts', flowing from the three divine persons, but the divine substance remains entirely transcendent and incommunicable, the totally mysterious, indescribable reality shared by the persons. In its context, this was an important bulwark against a destructively rationalist party in the Byzantine Church; it was a theory allowing for authentic sharing in the divine life, while maintaining God's transcendence of all creaturely knowledge and existence. However, it is fraught with serious logical problems, and it seems unlikely that Basil and Gregory (and other early writers who use such a distinction) had in mind so precise a picture. In their works, knowing God 'in His acts', his *energeiai* or *dynameis,* may mean several different things. It may refer to what we have been considering in the last few pages, knowing God by doing what he does; it may refer (as, for instance, in *de beat.* VI, 1268C–9A) to knowing God 'by analogy' through his created works – something like Origen's or Philo's 'natural' knowledge of God, the finding of him in the harmony of the created order; or it *may* refer to the 'glory' of God, the sense of a palpable presence (again, *de beat.* VI, possibly, and *de orat. dom.* II; on the 'glory' of God, *de vita Moysis,* 407A–C; though notice that this is immediately qualified by a reference to knowing God by following him in the life of virtue). None of these cases corresponds very convincingly with Palamas' usage; in spite of the persuasive arguments of many contemporary Eastern Orthodox scholars, I believe it is more helpful to understand Gregory of Nyssa's use of the distinction between substance and act in a far looser sense (and the same would hold for Basil, and for their colleague and friend, Gregory Nazianzen, who employs very similar language). The distinction goes back, in one form or another, to Philo and even earlier, and was obviously a helpful tool in securing a proper doctrine of transcendence; but its imprecise and *ad hoc* character should be recognized. For Gregory, its use is closely bound to the whole of his attitude towards the difference between conceptual and moral or relational knowledge of God. It cannot be made into a metaphysical thesis.

To share in true virtue is 'nothing else but to share in God' (*de vita Moysis* 301 A); but the nature of God is limitless. So 'the longing of someone so sharing in God stretches out towards what is boundless, and of necessity never comes to a halt' (ibid. B). If the Christian life is a journey into God, it is a journey into infinity – not an abstract 'absoluteness' but an infinity of what Gregory simply calls 'goodness', an infinite resource of mercy, help and delight. And because of its limitless nature, this journey is always marked by *desire,* by hope and longing, never coming to possess or control its object. This is perhaps Gregory's most vivid way of expressing the Christian conviction of God's transcendent freedom and objectivity: faith is *always,* not only in this life, a longing and trust directed away from itself towards an object to which it will never be adequate, which it will never comprehend. God is what we have not yet understood, the sign of a strange and unpredictable future. If one wants to use the word, it could be said that Gregory's conception is markedly 'eschatological', just as much as is the New Testament's view of faith – something turned towards a future which is in God's hands alone, living out of the future, out of what is not yet understood. To see, as Gregory does, the nature of man as characterized by longing is itself an important theological statement about humanity. Put this side by side with the familiar Greek Christian distinction between 'image' and 'likeness' of God in humanity, the possibility and the actuality of communion with God, and it is very clear that a consistent and powerful understanding of humanity emerges from the thought of the Greek Fathers. Human nature is seen as *essentially* restless, precarious, mobile and variegated, because of its orientation towards a reality outside itself. The movement of history and of biography is made possible and meaningful by its reference to God who meets us *in* history, yet extends beyond it, is always, so to speak, ahead of it. Here if anywhere are the foundations for a Christian account both of history and of human individuality. This is Christianity's major revision of the philosophical assumptions of Greek antiquity.

The pilgrimage must begin, then, with the stirring of desire. The movement of faith does not arise 'by fear or by natural necessity, but by the desire and longing to share in what is good' (*in cant.* I. 768C), and so is awakened by beauty (ibid. cf. *de virginitate,* PG. 46. 360c–364A). God must illuminate and attract by his revelation. Thus, in the *Life of Moses,* Gregory writes of the burning bush as a symbol of the incarnation; through the miracle of the virginal conception, 'the light of the Godhead shone upon human life' (*de vita Moysis* 332D). And as the vision of the burning bush is the beginning of the liberation of the Hebrews from bondage, so the vision of the true light incarnate in the flesh of Jesus is the beginning of our liberation from sin's tyranny (ibid. 333 CD). What the incarnation effects for humanity Gregory understands very much in terms of 'recapitulation'. We have already noted what he has to say about Christ's poverty, and his argument against Eunomius that God must penetrate the entirety of human experience if he is to transform. Thus we read, to take one passage out of very many, that, 'since what was required was that the whole of nature should be raised up again from death, He stretched out His hand to the body laid out for burial; and having thereby bent down to our corpse He drew near to death, so as to lay hold on our mortal state and give to this mortal nature a beginning of the resurrection through His own body, raising up in power with Himself the whole man' (*or.catechetica* 32). So the dawning of our liberation (as for Irenaeus) is the demonstration in the flesh of the transformation of worldly human existence, including suffering and death. This is the 'beauty' which draws us and which we, like Moses, must preach.

The Hebrews, however, did not hear Moses' preaching with any enthusiasm. The call to freedom is a harsh and menacing thing as well as a promise and a hope. The 'enemy of human kind', seeing that the desire of men and women is kindled by the offer of freedom, at once presses down with doubts and temptations; and these assaults, which are for some an occasion of growth and strengthening, are for many simply a cause of fear, and the devil succeeds in preventing them from 'raising their eyes to heaven', (ibid. 341 CD). The believer is called to exercise his freedom – once again, to *create* his life – in the arena of moral struggle, temptation and uncertainity, and this is a vocation requiring trust and courage and a readiness to confront the wilderness which lies ahead. This brief passage is distantly reminiscent of Dostoyevsky's 'Parable of the Grand Inquisitor' in *The Brothers Karamazov*: the Inquisitor, like the devil of the temptation narratives in the Gospels and of Gregory's text, knows all too well that the passion for freedom in human hearts is balanced by the passion for security and, like the Israelites 'making accusations against those who promised them deliverance from slavery' (341 D), accuses Christ of failing to know what is the deepest need of man and offering a freedom which human beings cannot bear.

But in those who do respond to the promise, God acts painfully and drastically: the death of the Egyptian firstborn is to be understood as the cutting off in us of the roots of sin, of sinful appetites (ibid. 353 BC). It is the beginning, therefore, of the reordering of our desires heavenwards. And although it is a kind of death, the real life of the soul is preserved by the blood of the 'true lamb', the Christian Paschal victim, Jesus crucified. This happens by night; and by night the Israelites leave Egypt, travelling in the 'cloud' which is 'the grace of the Holy Spirit . . . through Whom comes into being the assurance of liberty' (361B). The passing of the Red Sea, of course, represents our baptism (361 D ff) – death, new life, the sealing with the Spirit and an entry into a life lived through the victory of the cross. This victory is soon demonstrated when the 'bitter waters' of pain and uncertainty are made 'sweet' by the casting into them of the wood of the cross (365 AB); and it is also symbolized in the battle with the Amalekites, when Moses holds up his arms all day long to secure the victory of Israel (371 BC). In spite of all the considerable emphasis on struggle and decision in Gregory's writing, there is no suggestion that this is or ever can be the achievement of unaided human will: the advance becomes possible only by conscious commitment to the model of Christ's life-in-death and by calling upon the resources of the Spirit in whom Jesus endures and offers, without whom there is no 'assurance of liberty', no hope.

So the people of God advance towards Sinai, the mountain of God, towards the vision of 'the transcendent nature (373 AB). At Sinai, all the animals have to be kept away from the mountain, on pain of death; so must all that is purely 'animal' in the human spirit be put aside here. The knowledge of sense experience is 'animal' in the sense that it is all the brute creation is capable of: it is not *distinctively* human, and the ascent to God is concerned with nothing if not the human (ibid. CD). Here Gregory sounds a familiar Hellenic and Platonic note, exhorting the believer to put aside all that is sub-rational. But in what follows, all trace of 'intellectualism' is thoroughly purged. Gregory, more than any of his predecessors, refuses any ultimate privilege to the *nous* as such in the knowledge of God: it is as much creaturely as the body and the passions, and so as much in need of transformation. This is made clear in the theme of alternation of light and darkness which Gregory uses in describing the ascent of God. Religious knowledge begins with illumination (as we have seen in the image of the burning bush), the putting away of the destructive and imprisoning darkness (*skotos*) of sin. Illumination and 'godliness', *eusebeia,* are one and the same at this stage (375 CD). But as the soul or *nous* grows and progresses, it becomes more and more evident that the divine nature is *atheoretos,* 'not-to-be-looked-on': there is no illumination that can make the human subject capable of such a vision. Not only sense knowledge but discursive reason must yield at this stage. The only *dianoia*, 'understanding', of God of which man is capable is 'not-seeing', the acceptance, in faith and trust, of the human subject's feebleness before God. 'No one has ever seen God'; the divine substance, what-it-is-to-be-God, is beyond any kind of intellection. Thus Moses, when he goes to meet God, goes into the cloud that covers Sinai, climbing 'always higher' (377 C).

This is a passage of such great importance that it is worth pausing on for a while. The idea that God, or the supreme being, or the Idea of the Good, was above 'being' was common in classical philosophy: Plato twice makes such a statement (in *Parmenides* 137C–142A and *Republic* 509C). The point is that the One or the Good is the source of all definable, limited things, and this cannot itself be a 'thing', subject to limit and determination. It is not *a* being, nor can it be said to have an 'essence', in the sense of having a definition. This in itself is not all original to Gregory; writers like Philo and Origen had said much the same. However, the Platonic tradition had generally assumed that the intellect, when sufficiently purified, led back from the multiplicity of things to pure simplicity, would naturally 'gravitate' to its proper 'home' in the transcendent. Plotinus, the great neo-Platonic writer of the third century, had spoken of the 'ecstasy' in which the *nous* escaped its own limited and material bondage to fly back to the One in an intermittent experience of mystical absorption. Gregory, however, makes the *nous* homeless again: it is not a simple matter of stripping away impediments to the flight to the absolute. When all that is non-rational is put aside, and the soul or intellect is naked before God, it confronts a stranger: the uncreated Lord is still and always will be on the far side of an unbridgeable gulf, and the soul will not ever be able to rest in the security of perfect union in the Platonic sense. Plato, Philo and Plotinus would all agree that the soul cannot express God in image or concept; it is Gregory who grounds this incapacity in a *metaphysical* gulf between God and the created self. And if this grounding is correct, the soul's momentary ecstasy is something of an irrelevancy. What matters is the *epektasis* of love and longing, permeating the whole of life. The substance of God is not to be touched or known; it is an abstraction and, in a sense, a fantasy; there is no core of the divine being to be grasped as the final, 'essential' quality of God, only the divine works, God willing to relate to the world in love. These works or operations are equally inaccessible to conceptualizing, simply because they are known only by being experienced, by the character of a life lived out of them and in their strength.

On the summit of the mountain, Moses was shown a 'tabernacle not made with hands' as the model for the tabernacle he was to construct below. This tabernacle, in which the power and wisdom of God are displayed to men and dwell with them, is Christ (381AB). In other words,what Moses is permitted to *see* on the mountain is not, as it might be in a strict Platonic scheme, a 'realm of ideas', but the first and greatest of God's acts, his self-communication in Christ. Yet Moses presses forward; the encounter with Christ as the wellspring of God's self-giving is not a stopping-point (401B). He is warned that man cannot see the face of God and live; and Gregory interprets this very ingeniously and unexpectedly by denying that the sight of God can itself be fatal and suggesting that the meaning is that God's 'face', that which can be seen of God, is, on its own, less than life-giving. To be content with the 'face' of God is to be content with less than God (401D – 403B). Once again, all trace of an external and static relationship between God and believer is expunged. Even to behold Christ is not life-giving, unless it is supplemented by something further. And this 'something further' is explained in the curious passage where Moses is described as seeing the 'back parts' of God. Here too, Gregory's exegesis is unusual. Moses is set 'upon the rock' to see God passing by, and the rock is, predictably, Christ; but, we are told, Moses sees God's back because he is *following* God, borne up upon his shoulders (407AC). He sees all around God's 'glory', called by various names in Scripture – the Kingdom of Heaven, the New Jerusalem, and so forth, and this seems to mean something like the diffused sense of God's presence, or of God's directing hand. But what lies ahead is God's back, the figure of the Lord leading us further and further out of self into his own country and his own life. It is a striking picture, perhaps not least because of its New Testament resonances: 'And they were on the road, going up to Jerusalem, and Jesus was walking ahead of them; and they were amazed, and those who followed were afraid' (Mark 10.32). That and kindred texts must surely have formed part of the complex of resources and influences behind this passage of Gregory's.

The vision of God *is* discipleship. Gregory states this as clearly as possible in this section of the *Vita*. The following of God with all one's heart and soul and powers is to see God (409), and the end of virtuous life is to be and to be called (like Moses) God's 'household servant' (472D). Yet the believer is more than a servant; God spoke to Moses as a man to his friend (Exod.33.11) and the Christian is also *friend* of God. Such friendship is identical with 'the perfection of life' (429C); we return here to the theme of perfection introduced at the very beginning of the *Vita*, to see it in all its fulness – not as a static 'achievement', but as a condition of human existence fulfilled in intimacy of relationship with God. Gregory keeps scrupulously within the limits of his text here, and has, surprisingly, nothing to say about the Christian's relation to God as Father in this final stage. But that this was a theme of importance to him is clear (as we have earlier seen) from the works on the Lord's Prayer and the Beatitudes. Another theme of significance receives a brief mention in the closing paragraphs of the *Vita*, when Gregory describes the mature believer, the incorruptibility (472D). The 'image', here as in the other ascetical works we have mentioned, is rooted in a moral and relational conception of the Christian life. 'To have

God within oneself' (*de beatitudinibus,* VI.1269C), to 'imitate the divine nature' (*de or. dominica* V.1180C; and cf. *de professione christiana*, PG. 46, 244C.), to be restored in the image of God, is consistently to follow the pattern of God's life as revealed in Jesus. On the last day, we shall be judged according to our compassion, not our knowledge or any other achievement (*de beat.*V.*passim*).

The Problem of Platonism

Vladimir Lossky, in his important work on the Eastern spiritual tradition, *The Vision of God,* has said that, for Gregory, 'the celestial journey of the soul . . . is interiorized' (p.72). Putting it in other terms, we might say that the inherited Platonic scheme of the soul's flight from the world is demythologized – even that the soul itself is demythologized. The drama of the alien soul flying from the bondage of the senses is replaced by the very different 'drama' of soul and senses together struggling to live into and assimilate a truth greater than themselves. Cardinal Daniélou (introducing his anthology of extracts from Gregory, *From Glory to Glory,* translated by H. Musurillo) has rightly said that Gregory effects a 'revolution in thought' by denying the classical equation of change with evil and inmutability with good (pp.47–8). If human beings are not simply composed of a potentially timeless and transcendent soul and an imprisoning body, but are limited and contingent in soul as well as body, salvation cannot be neatly reduced to the sorting out of one element from the other. The soul's only security is in change. As Gregory says in the *Vita* (407 CD), this is one of the great paradoxes of faith, that faithfulness in virtue is the principle of change; while, without change, there is no stability in perfection. To stop growing and changing is to fall away from stability. None of this is at all a revelling in paradox for its own sake. As we have seen, it is an integral part of what may without too much anachronism be called a 'personalist' rather than an intellectualist view of the Christian life, in which concepts of vocation and choice play a significant role. It is a view, like the views of Ignatius and Irenaeus, which st the creative – *making* one's life, making one's soul, in a ce fashion, deciding, developing, intending and desiring, in operation, *synergeia*, with God. It combines a profound p-simism about natural endowments and natural knowledge with a profound optimism about the freedom of the human will when enlightened and enriched by the life of God, the will which (as in Irenaeus' theology) Christ restores to its proper and creative dignity.

Any system which emphasizes the role and the capacity of the will inevitably runs some risk of a kind of moralism, a Stoic rather than a Christian preoccupation with right choice and right action, in which penitence and grace play little part. Gregory avoids this by stressing the absolute dependence of Christian freedom upon the illumination and recreation of Christ's work. If occasionally, in the *Vita Moysis* or, even more, in earlier works like the *de beatitudinibus*, the emphasis on virtuous life or purity seems far removed from a Pauline gospel of sin and redemption, it should be remembered that Gregory is always speaking of the humanity refashioned by the incarnate life of Christ, 'passing through the whole range of our poverty' (*de beat.* I. 1201C). Natural humanity is in need of grace and of liberation; that is the whole burden of the *Vita*. When set free, human nature has overwhelming possibilities precisely because it is now taking on the shape sketched by Christ. It may be worth noting too that Gregory lays little stress on *apatheia:* passion is not in itself sin, and the virtuous man will not try to eradicate passion but will seek to control and direct it properly (*de beat.* II. 1216A–1217D, VI. 1271D–end), finding what its good uses may be. The 'passionate' in human nature, then, is not outside the scope of salvation; the human ideal is not the extirpation of 'inferior' faculties, but a controlled and integrated use of all that is human. And Gregory, like most of his contemporaries, believed that the sacrament of the Eucharist united the body to Christ, conferring incorruptibility upon it (*oratio catechetica*, XXXVII); the Eucharist is, as for Ignatius, a bodily medicine in a fairly straightforward sense. Crude as this may seem to some modern taste, there is a very important affirmation here about the Christian destiny of the body, an implicitly strong valuation of the life of the flesh: the spiritual journey is not 'interiorized' in the sense that it is withdrawn from the public and corporate. To share physically in the Lord's Supper, to receive Christ in the midst of his Church, is indispensable to the life of grace, ensuring that it does not shrink to the dimensions of private spiritual experience. So Gregory completes the articulation of a Christian reply to any form of gnostic dualism and esotericism. Throughout his work, the new Christian picture of human being is drawn with subtlety and exactness, the picture of a humanity no less tragically divided than in the classical Hellenic model, yet called forward out of sin and self to an unimaginable wholeness in that knowledge of God which is the following of Christ in inexhaustible love and longing.

Gregory's picture is clearer even than those of his great contemporaries, his brother Basil and their friend Gregory Nazianzen. Indeed, Nazianzen, while sharing a great deal of Gregory's scheme and presenting it with a personal fervour and poignancy not often found in Gregory, retains a certain degree of 'Origenist' spiritualism. In his *Orationes XL* and *XLI,* on baptism, the emphasis is more on vision and intellectual illumination than on simple relationship; and in *Oratio XXVIII,* the second 'theological oration', there is a considerable use of pure Platonic imagery – shadows and substance (3), the 'darkness of the body' (12) and so on. Yet in the same work (4), he decisively parts company with Plato: Plato had said that it was difficult to conceive God, but impossible to express him; and Nazianzen turns this on its head by insisting that if God is impossible to *express,* he cannot be conceived at all. So, like Gregory of Nyssa, he denies that anyone can ever know the nature or essence of God (17): the only names which can be given to this nature are 'He Who is', or simply 'God' (*Oratio XXX* 18–19) – terms which express no concept we can give real content to. Nazianzen is, as Lossky points out, deeply concerned about the vision of God being the vision of the Trinity; and, again as Lossky says (op.cit.,p.70), it is hard to see what exactly this means. As he normally expresses it, it seems to represent a retreat from the strongly relational trinitarianism of Athanasius, even of Origen, towards a threefold *object* of contemplation. The earlier writers had understood participation in the Trinity as a sharing in the Son's relation to the Father; Nazianzen envisages a union with the whole of the threefold reality which is set 'over against us'. Lossky says, accurately, that the vision of the Trinity in Nazianzen corresponds to the vision of the divine substance in Hellenic mysticism; but to say this is to put a large question-mark against Nazianzen's trinitarianism. The original strength of trinitarianism (in Athanasius, Gregory, and many passages of Nazianzen himself) lay in its intimate connection with the doctrine of salvation – becoming 'sons in the Son'. Nazianzen, with his marked fondness for speaking of the soul contemplating *the Trinity,* is in danger of cutting the doctrine off from its real roots and reverting to the simple human subject – divine object antithesis which earlier Christian writers had sought so hard to modify.

The results of this are visible in the writings of Nazianzen's pupil and friend, Evagrius of Pontus (346–99), one of the most significant spiritual writers in the Eastern ascetical tradition. Despite his posthumous condemnation for 'Origenism', his works were widely read and transcribed under the names of other writers (the treatise *de oratione* was long ascribed to Nilus of Sinai). Evagrius adopts the now familiar distinction between 'natural', 'practical' and 'theological' stages in Christian life used by Origen, Gregory of Nyssa and others, and one of his major surviving treatises is the *Capita practica,* dealing with the second level. The 'practical' is, he says, 'the spiritual method by which the passionate part of the soul (*psyche*) is purified' (*cap.*L,1230A); the goal of the 'practical' life, the life of ascetic struggle, is *apatheia,* the marks of which are carefully enumerated (*cap.*XXXV – XLII, 1231A–C). And at the very beginning of this treatise, Evagrius says that 'The Kingdom of Heaven is *apatheia* of soul (*psyche*), together with the true knowledge of things', and that 'The Kingdom of God is *gnosis* of the Holy Trinity, extending to the whole constitution of the soul (*nous*)' (*cap.* II and III, 1221D). The distinction between *psyche* and *nous* is related to Origen's view that the empirical soul with its sinful passions is the fallen form of *nous,* pure intellect. The purpose of prayer is the restoration of *nous.* At the beginning of *de* *oratione,* we read that 'The *psyche* which has been purified by the fullness of the virtues makes the structure of the *nous* immovable, rendering it fit for the condition which it seeks', and this is followed by the definition of prayer as the 'conversation' or 'speech' of the *nous* to or with God (*cap.*II and III,1167C). Thus, prayer properly so called follows upon *praktike*; when *apatheia* is attained, 'love' results ('Love is the child of *apatheia'; cap. pract.* LIII, 1233B), and this love is the gateway to gnosis. Love, for Evagrius, is essentially love of knowledge, pure devotion to and desire for the illumination of God in the soul (v. *Capita Gnostica. Cent.* IV.50). It is what leads to the state in which the soul is filled with divine light, understanding itself in its true character as the dwelling-place of God (e.g., *Cap. Gnost. Cent.* III. 6). The 'naked soul' is reunited to the primordial simplicity of God.

Evagrius leaves no room for Gregory of Nyssa's vision of progress into darkness; for him, as for Nazianzen, ignorance is bad – any kind of ignorance, at any stage. It is an elementary and transitory stage, the condition of the unilluminated spirit. And if the spirit's home or true nature is in God, there can be no sense of that lack of 'fit' between *nous* and God which we have seen to be central for Gregory. Antoine and Claire Guillaumont, whose work on Evagrius has revealed the outlines of his work and thought more clearly than ever before, write that, in Evagrius' ascetical doctrine, 'the human situation, man's position between demons and angels, is nothing other than a phase in the cosmic history of Intellect, returning to unity after its fall' (*Reallexikon für Antike und Christentum,* vol. 6, art. 'Evagrius Ponticus', col. 1101). After its brief but dramatic 'exile from the land of unity' in Gregory of Nyssa, the soul is reinstated in full Platonic dignity. Gregory's eccentricity becomes all the clearer when he is compared with an Evagrius.

Here again, in the fourth as in the second century, we may see Christian thought retreating from the strangeness of its own implications into a comfortable metaphysical harbour. The flight from contingency triumphs; Evagrius is profoundly concerned with the fight against temptations and passions, but the goal is extirpation, not integration, the *reduction* of the human subject. Gregory in effect argues for the expansion of the human subject in encounter with God – by means of a far-reaching stripping and purgation certainly, but a purgation designed precisely to allow for growth. Evagrius points us back to the motionless and timeless stability of eternal Understanding and has little to say concerning those moral and public corollaries of faith in which Gregory was so interested. Evagrius, *agape* is a stepping-stone to *gnosis*; Gregory's *epithymia,* longing, is what abides when 'knowledge' is seen to be an illusory dream. Gregory's definition of human nature as 'self-transcending' ensures that knowledge of God can only be seen as personal, relational, evolving, a *project* for human life. It does not culminate in 'vision' but in the love of servant, friend, disciple and, ultimately, child; its contemplative gaze is something both receptive and responsive, an attention which is content not to understand nor in any way possess. Evagrius' terminology and many of his assumptions – particularly the notion of 'pure prayer', the unimpeded direction of the soul to God – came to permeate much of the Christian mystical and ascetical tradition and proved rich and fertile resources. But only when combined with and questioned by something resembling Gregory's view of human nature could they survive as a vehicle for *Christian* prayer. The incarnational paradox, God in flesh, 'raising up in power with Himself the whole man', leaves us with an inescapably 'restless spirituality, always liable to criticism and change – not exactly an 'iconoclastic' spirituality, but one charged with a systemic *suspicion* of images and concepts of God, the world and self. Evagrius' may be an 'imageless' prayer; but we need Gregory's scepticism to prevent imageless prayer itself from becoming an idol, a stopping point. And yet, though the soul is homeless and vulnerable, in deserts and clouds, it is most importantly 'at home' in so far as God *has* made Himself a home in human life and death, and passed before us on the way we are called to go. Christ is the root of our security and our insecurity alike, promise and judgement, end and beginning, the burning bush, the Paschal lamb, the rock and the tabernacle, present as a sign of hope at every stage of our painful journey out of bondage and across the wilderness.

4. The Clamour of the Heart

When, in 401, Augustine of Hippo, bishop, celebrated theologian and controversialist, preacher, ascetic, spiritual director, published ten books of *Confessions,* he was not indulging in a taste for literary self-congratulation or self-advertisement. As Peter Brown has emphasized in his magnificent study, *Augustine of Hippo* (ch.16), this was a new *kind* of book. It was a work in which the writer's struggles were worked out on the written page, in which a meaningful life had to be created in words. Augustine is never merely remembering; he is searching for significant patterns, *making* a biography. Again and again the questions recur. *Why* was this so? Where is the hand of God in this or that experience? And yet the question repeatedly modulates into a different key; not, Where was God? but, Where was I? 'But where was I when I was seeking You? You were there in front of me, but I had wandered away from myself. And if I could not find my own self, how much less could I find You? (V.2). So much of the *Confessions* centres upon the image of homecoming. God waits for the soul to come back to its home with him; without that home in God, nothing can have any meaning. 'What it is that I want to say to You, Lord God, is nothing but this, that I do not know where I came from into this world, into this – what should I say? – this deathly life, this living death; no, I do not know' (I.6). Identity is ultimately in the hand of God; but this does not mean that it is a non-temporal thing. It is to be found, and in some sense *made,* by the infinitely painstaking attention to the contingent strangeness of remembered experience in conscious reference to God which makes up most of this extraordinary work. Augustine, says Peter Brown (op.cit., p.164), 'distils a new feeling' from the memory of uncomprehended emotion. The light of God can make a story, a continuous reality, out of the chaos of unhappiness, 'homeless' wandering, hurt and sin. And so nothing can be left out of account – not even the very first inklings of experience, the origin of consciousness itself. Augustine shows a wholly new concern with childhood experiences and a new understanding of their determinative importance. His field of study is, uncomprisingly, the whole mental history of human beings.

As for so many of the Greek Fathers, and the Neo-Platonic philosophers who so influenced his early development, Augustine sees the fall of man as a fall from unity. But it is considered less a fall from a primordial, absolute One than a fall from the experienced harmony of self with self and self with God. Gregory of Nyssa had denied the soul a 'home' with God in the sense of a natural kinship; Augustine reaffirms that the soul is at home only in God, because there alone is it itself, in the love and knowledge of God, held in his hand. There is no contradiction here, for Augustine has moved a good way from a simple Neo-Platonic monism and has little to say of natural kinship between God and the soul. 'Our good lives with You, without anything lacking, because our good is You Yourself. And we shall not be afraid that there is no longer anywhere we can return to, because we fell from our place: we may be far away, but our home does not fall into ruin. It is Your own eternity' (IV.16). To be at home is not to vanish into an impersonal cosmic unity, but to rediscover the eternal, patient, faithful love of our creator, who made us to enjoy him, so that 'our hearts are restless till they come to rest in You' (I.1). And to be thus at home is to know oneself in knowing God: 'What I do know of myself I know because You shed Your light on me; and what I do not know of myself I know because You shed Your light on me; and what I do not know of myself I shall still not know until "my darkness shall become as noonday" in the vision of Your face' (X.5). In so far as we can look at our lives and see more than chaos we have come nearer our home in God; in so far as we are still bewildered, lost, guilty and afraid, we are not at home, not in harmony. Book X of the *Confessions* is a particularly passionate and moving declaration of what it is to be on the way and not yet arrived at journey's end. It is a statement of the pain and labour of a life of unfulfilled desire, the stumbling advance towards that beauty whose compelling force first broke through the defences of the soul, drew it out and set it on its pilgrimage – the vision, clear for a few rare and indescribably precious moments, never quite lost, awaking the ache of longing which nothing else will ever again satisfy. It is worth quoting in full the unforgettable twenty-seventh chapter of Book X:

> How late I came to love You, O beauty so ancient and so fresh, how late I came to love You! You were within me while I had gone outside to seek you. Unlovely myself, I rushed towards all those lovely things You had made. And always You were with me, and I was not with You. All these beauties kept me far from you – although they would not have existed at all unless they had their being in You. You called, You cried, You shattered my deafness. You sparkled, You blazed, You drove away my blindness. You shed Your fragrance, and I drew in my breath, and I pant for You. I tasted and now I hunger and thirst. You touched me, and now I burn with longing for your peace.

As Book X goes on to set out in merciless detail, the quest and the longing for God's beauty are inextricably bound to the struggle with temptations of body and spirit, the progressive purification of all experience. Conversion is a beginning, not an end, an entry into a perilous and confused world. 'In all these dangers and strugglings and others like them, You see the shuddering of my heart. I feel not so much that I do not suffer from my wounds as that they are being healed by You time and time again' (x.39). The outcome of the Christian enterprise is uncertain: in the struggle between the miseries of evildoing and the joys of goodness, 'I do not know to which side victory will fall' (x.28). Because the believer is set in the midst of vast and uncontrollable realities, because he is hidden from himself, liable to disastrous illusions, because the human spirit is a dark and irrational place, there can be no safe predictions. Belief does not confer *hesychia,* the repose of the gnostic; it is the heartbreaking source of human unrest, 'echoed ecstasy/Not lost, but requiring, pointing to the agony/ Of death and birth' (T.S. Eliot, *East Coker,* 131–3), the vision always *to be* found and realized in the ambivalent and tormented flesh.

The Call of Desire

Augustine is less concerned than almost any of the Greek Fathers with freedom. For Gregory of Nyssa, the 'surd' element, the unpredictable and unconceptualizable, in human life, is the mysterious depth of the spirit itself, awakened by grace to become what it should be, the resource of freedom from which the life of virtue is continually being constructed. The human will and its longing when turned to their proper object can direct the potentially destructive, arbitrary, anarchic freedom of men and women into selfless and loving action. As we have already seen, the Greek writers are typically concerned with the eradication or, more realistically, control of the 'passions'; the end of the life of grace is a condition in which behaviour is no longer determined by passion, that is, by irrational impulse. The ideal is a life whose development is a matter of elected and willed construction. Augustine, however, moves further and further away from such a model as his thought matures. For him, the 'surd' is not so much a dimension of the spirit itself as the enormous world of pressures and influences in the midst of which the spirit lives. The human subject is indeed a mystery; no one could be more painfully and eloquently aware of this than Augustine. But the mysteriousness and unpredictability have more to do with the forces which act on the subject; and this is true both inside and outside the life of grace. More and more, Augustine treats human activity as grounded in some sort of compulsion: rational freedom of choice recedes into the distant background. The struggle with Pelagius and his followers which clouded his later years drives him to state ever more sharply the helplessness of the human spirit, the battleground of powerful supra-human forces. His doctrine of predestination emerges as the logical climax of a long pilgrimage away from the Hellenic optimism which could envisage some sort of complete rational direction of the darkness of the heart.

Augustine's undiminished appeal to a post-Freudian generation has much to do with this aspect of his thought. He confronts and accepts the unpalatable truth that rationality is not the most important factor in human experience, that the human subject is a point in a vast structure of forces whose operation is entirely obscure to the reason. Human reality is acted upon at least as much as acting. The heart is moved, drawn, tossed about by impulse and desire, and 'will' has less to do with reason than with passion. In his discussion of will in the *The City of God (de civ. Dei* XIV.6), Augustine says plainly that the 'motions of the soul' are identical with what we mean by 'will': 'What is desire or gladness but a willing in accord with the things we want? What is fear or sorrow but a willing in discord with the things we do *not* want? When we consent to the quest for what we want, that is desire, and when we consent to the enjoyment of what we want, that is what we call gladness.' Will is the reception of impulse into the conscious mind: a will divorced from impulse is unthinkable. Thus Augustine can treat the notion of *apatheia* with considerable reserve. If it refers to the absence of those impulses which are of their nature inimical to judgement and harmony, it is something to be aimed at, although never to be attained on earth; if it suggests an absence of all *affectus,* all emotional life, it is 'worse than sin' (XIV.9). Sorrow, fear, compassion, love, delight are the very stuff of moral and spiritual life: did not Christ experience them all fully and really? Those who fancy they have put emotion behind them 'have lost the fulness of their humanity rather than attaining real peace' (ibid.). 'Do you imagine, brothers,' he asks his congregation at Hippo, 'that people who fear God . . . have no emotions?' (*en. in Ps.*76.14). 'Do not try to keep your soul free from emotional influences' (*en. in Ps.* 55.6).

Salvation, then, has little or nothing to do with the enthronement of reason over the passions. Human beings are naturally passionate, vulnerable, mobile, and if their humanity is to be saved it must be without loss of all this. So, returning to the *Confessions* we may see more plainly the deep pastoral interest undergirding the whole work. Augustine describes and analyses the insecurity of his present experience and the confusion of his past experience so as to give the lie to any pious rhetoric about the life of grace which might drive the weak to despair. 'When they read or hear these confessions of my past sins, which You have forgiven and over which you have drawn a veil, so as to give me bliss in You, transforming my soul by faith and sacrament, then their hearts will be aroused. They will no longer lie in the slumber of despair, saying, "I cannot", but will awake in the love of Your mercy, tasting the sweetness of Your grace' (X.3). The *Confessions* provide a unique testimony to the fact that it is God and God alone who can give shape and meaning to a human life. The struggles of men and women to make their own lives and build their own securities end in despair; and this is equally true for the believer and the unbeliever. Conversion does not signify an end to the chaos of human experience, it does not make self-understanding suddenly easy or guarantee an ordered or intelligible life. What is changed in conversion is the set of determinants within which the spirit moves; and these may be as inaccessible to the mind as they were before. Thus the confidence of the believer never rests upon either his intellectual grasp or his intellectual control of his experience, but on the fidelity of the heart's longing to what has been revealed as the only finally satisfying object of its desire. Of course it would be wrong to take this as meaning that Augustine subscribes to pure irrationalism. On the contrary, every page he wrote witnesses to his consuming passion for *truth,* vision and clarity, and we have noted what he has to say in the *City of God* about passions that obscure the exercise of *ratio.* But the clear, 'unillusioned' rationality which Augustine seeks is a candour about the human condition and its needs which is courageous enough to see and admit and accept the frailty of its own foundation. We are pointed back to the central theme of the *Confessions:* the 'making of a biography' by attention to experience *in the light of God.* Rationality looks honestly at its own human location and finds doubt and confusion, a dark abyss. To find its own truth it must look beyond.

Even in the *Confessions,* Augustine's Platonic background leads him on occasion to use language which, to some ears, has an 'intellectualist' ring. In the great account of Augustine's and Monica's shared ecstasy at Ostia, shortly before the latter's death, Augustine speaks of touching the eternal Wisdom of God *rapida cogitatione,* 'in a moment's fleeting thought' (IX.10.iii). Yet the whole tenor of this passage has far more to do with the life of the heart than with that of the reason: the first time Augustine speaks of the ecstatic experience here (10.ii) he describes it as attained *ictu cordis,* 'with the piercing glance of the *heart*'! Essentially, it is the heart – or, sometimes, the 'understanding' (*mens*) – which is the subject of religious knowledge, never the discursive reason. Before ever God can be spoken of, the heart must 'imagine' or 'figure' him, and 'recognize' him as its resting place; and it grows in this exercise by approaching and growing like him in a life of charity (*en. in Ps.* 99.6); the closeness of this to Gregory of Nyssa's view is notable). God is not known by *scientia* but by *sapientia,* the contemplative turning towards the object, not the active intellect at work on the object, organizing and analysing (the distinction is discussed in Books XII to XIV of the *de Trinitate;* and see pp. 60–73 of John Burnaby's superb essay, *Amor Dei*). And contemplative knowledge can be only the knowledge of love, of desire and delight, the will consenting to the drawing of the divine beauty.

The *beauty* of God, 'so ancient and so fresh', is a constant theme of Augustine's. It is the vision of an indescribable loveliness that calls our hearts out of darkness, breaking down the barriers of false love, rightly ordering those desires and impulses by which we live. In the *City of God* (XV.22), Augustine quotes from the Song of Songs (2.4): 'He has set love in order in me.' This offers a 'short and accurate definition of virtue', as *ordered* love, love which recognizes and clings to what is authentically lovable and is not content with merely transient beauties. Created beauty and created good can never be rightly loved *as ends in themselves;* the earthly city struggles for peace and harmony, and these ends are good, and the struggle is worth undertaking; but its gains are fragile and its risks great (ibid. IV.4). It was Cain who built the first city: it was the first murderous despiser of God who built an earthly *home* while Abel remained a 'pilgrim' (ibid.XV.1). The city of man, the *civitas terrena,* is built in self-love, out of the human desire to make order and intelligibility and rest upon their achievement. 'And so two kinds of love have constructed the two cities: the earthly city, built by love of self leading to contempt of God, the heavenly city by love of God leading to contempt of self' (ibid.XIV.28). The earthly city is built by those who are confident of their control, not only over their individual biographies but over the whole human world. And this attitude Augustine rejects as fiercely in the social as in the individual sphere. Social good *is* good, peace and justice are to be sought with passion; but with 'ordered' passion, with the recognition that they are not to be considered as signs of human glory, human authority, human capacity to tame the world. They are sought because in them is seen something of God. If sought and 'enjoyed', loved for their own sake rather than 'used', directed to a greater end (Augustine elaborates the distinction in *de doctrina Christiana* I.4; see Burnaby, pp.105–7), their precariousness is at once obvious, and destructive misery follows for those who put their trust in them (*de civ.Dei* XV.4). Those who look for a home of human making secure only their own deepest alienation and homelessness. Only in God is there total faithfulness, total stability (*en. in Ps.* 41.12, and *Ps.* 121.6).

Yet it remains true what we learn about beauty – and so about desire – from earthly and passing beauties, and Augustine does not seek to devalue them. 'Starting from all those things which we love here, let us long all the more for Him' (*en. in Ps.* 84.9). If creation is beautiful, how much more lovely its creator must be (*en. in Ps.* 39.8, *Ps.* 79.14, *Ps.* 84.9, *Ps.* 85.9, etc)! and more, if the beauties of creation are sometimes overwhelming and terrifying, how much more must God's beauty be so (*in Ps.* 144.15)! 'If you can conceive anything more beautiful than God, so much the worse for your efforts at love' (*in Ps.* 43.16). The world's beauties are only God's 'engagement ring' for us; and who would be so foolish as to forgo the joys of marriage for the sake of the engagement ring (*in Ep. Joann.* 2.11)? All good, all beauty points away from itself to the source of all goodness, God, 'the Good that makes things good' (*in Ps.* 133.4), the Beauty that makes things beautiful. Augustine can even allow (*Serm.* 159.2) that 'the embraces of marriage' count among the earthly glories which point to God; a remarkable concession in a man for whom sexuality was, on the whole, a tormenting and destructive area of experience. All beauty, in some degree, pierces our blindness and deafness, leads us away from the dominating, organizing life of the intellect; in its alarming and overpowering character (and Augustine thinks here especially of spectacular 'natural' beauties), it is a standing challenge to the human fantasy of a world of controlled intelligibility. In his last works against the Pelagian Julian of Eclanum, Augustine points again and again to the oddity of the world, its irreducibility to the tidy patterns of logic (see Brown, *Augustine,* pp. 416–17). Like Gregory writing against Eunomius, he is profoundly concerned to demonstrate the inaccessibility of even the world of sense experience to the reasoning process; but he is able to give far richer content to the sense of wonder involved by invoking the effects of beauty. Intellect and the world of unpredictable loveliness can never match; only the heart can properly respond, because the heart does not seek to control, only to enjoy, and so is mobile, flexible, sensitive to all the bewildering diversity of the world.

The heart does not look for an easy stability. Augustine again uses similar language to that of Gregory of Nyssa in describing the never-ceasing pilgrimage of the heart or spirit or *mens* (an important concept for Augustine, as including understanding and will or love together). Desire impels us on, so 'let us run, let us strain forward' (*en. in Ps.* 38.6); for 'the only way you can be perfect in this life is by knowing that you cannot be perfect in this life' (ibid. 14). 'It is a great evil to have no hope in this life' (*en. in Ps.* 129.10). The heart is 'perfect' when it knows what it lacks (*in Ps.* 38.14), knows that there will be no resting place for it among the things of earth. To be in the way of salvation is to be dissatisfied, 'disquieted within', never complacent about your condition or secure in your understanding or your stable spiritual attainment (*in Ps.* 41.10–12). The psalmist says (in Augustine's Latin version), 'I poured out my soul *beyond* myself' (*super me*); that is where final delight is to be sought. The mystery of the depths of the self directs us beyond the world of clear and orderly sense experience but is itself only a stage on the road to the greater mystery of God: there is no substantial continuity between soul and God (*in Ps.* 41.7–8). So there is no rest in mere self-awareness, because to know the self properly is to see it set in the midst of the vast landscape of God's workings, a landscape with no human map, trusting only to the hand of God. Once having glimpsed this vastness and heard the distant sounds of the 'holiday of heaven' (ibid. 9), the spirit must live by hope, knowing as clearly as ever it will that nothing else can substitute for that vision and its delights.

Sharing the Cross

However, the compulsion towards the love of God's beauty comes not only from the loveliness but also from the horror of the world. The love of God looks in hope for fulfilment of a joy already begun, but also looks for the healing of the world's wounds; like all authentic hope, it is in some degree *protest*. Again, Augustine appears to become more and more painfully conscious of this with advancing age. Julian, Bishop of Eclanum, had suggested that life of unfallen man could not have been so very different from present human experience; and this and kindred assertions wring from Augustine a fierce and passionate denial. 'When he rounds on Julian for blandly defining away the extent of human unhappiness, we can at last sense an upsurge of genuine feeling, of moral outrage, a refusal to abandon hopes for something better, to deny unpleasant facts for the sake of intellectual comfort' (Brown, *Augustine*, p. 394). Repeatedly in his earlier works he insists that an incapacity to feel for and with the pains of others is a massive diminution of what it is to be human. The 'great price' paid by a person who does not feel sorrow in this life is 'monstrousness of soul and insensitivity of body' (*de. civ. Dei.* XIV. 9); and in the discourse on Psalm 41 (*en. in Ps.*

41.19) Augustine warns against any complacency in the face of the world's horrors. The more St Paul loved, the more he suffered on account of the sinfulness of others (*in Ps.* 98.13), and this is a model for us. The Christian needs to have more, not less exposed nerves than others to see the world with honesty enough to grasp its appalling cruelties.

'Out of the deep have I cried unto thee, O Lord.' And what else is that *profundum,* that abyss, but the whole of our present life (*in Ps.* 129.1). 'In the night-season did I sing of him', for 'it is only at night that He declares His pity' (*in Ps.* 41.16). 'Thy statutes have been my songs: in the house of my pilgrimage', and 'this "house of my pilgrimage" is the night-time . . . the night in which the hearts of men are hidden from each other' (*in Ps.* 118, xv.7–8). For one as preoccupied as Augustine with truth, candour, heart speaking to heart, what image could be more poignant? The world is not only a world of exhilarating mysteriousness, but one of agonizingly frustrating ignorance, a darkness in which human beings can never fully meet one another. The incomprehension with which we look upon the glories of the natural order is far more darkly shaded when we turn to the sufferings of men and women and the loneliness in which each must live. The *Confessions* return often to the theme of friendship and its immense importance in Augustine's life; yet here – almost in an 'aside' – is the mature man's judgement on the terrible, tantalizing inadequacy of human intimacy. The heart cannot even rest in the heart of another; and this is not the smallest of the incomprehensible griefs of human life.

To argue, as does Professor Burnaby in an uncharacteristically dismissive section of his great book (*Amor Dei,* pp. 201 ff), that Augustine has a fundamentally 'moralistic' view of human suffering (as purely therapeutic or educative) is to deny Augustine's constantly deepening sense of the tragic, the senseless, the irremediable in human pain. While he can certainly use the conventional language of suffering as a trial of faith, and so forth (e.g. *in Ps.* 66.3), there is evident, especially in the *Discourse on the Psalms,* a far more profound understanding, linked with the significance of the suffering and death of Christ. First and foremost, of course, the pain of the world is a sharp reminder that we must look elsewhere for our peace and our salvation, that God and his good gifts are not identical. We need constantly to be shown God's independence of the good and the beauty of this world, shown that the absence of earthly good and beauty does not of itself indicate the absence of their source. In the 'night of this world', our love towards God should be inflamed more and more by the signs of God's remoteness. We are called not to stoic resignation but to the purification of love and will. 'Be poor, then, so that your help is in God alone' (*in Ps.* 131.25): our pain uncovers for us our utter neediness, strips us naked before God, like Job (*in Ps.* 55.20, and *Ps.* 118. xi;5), drives us to doubt our own strength and power (*in Ps.* 46.3). In short, the sufferings of earthly life are not primarily designed to exercise our moral muscles, not even to teach us endurance, but are permitted by God so as to draw us to himself; they open our eyes to the true condition of finite existence, ours and the world's, the sphere of poverty, tears, loneliness, disillusion and the scars of countless unintelligible hurts. This is hardly 'moralism': it is a sombre picture of the way in which suffering shatters human security and forces us to confront irreducible reality in its least palatable shapes.

But this is not all. The assurance which upholds us in this poverty and need comes from the example of Christ. We find our own weakness in pain and dereliction, but are saved from despair by the knowledge of *Christ's* weakness. Christ suffers real mental anguish, sorrow and fear (*de. civ. Dei* XIV. 9, etc.) 'so that if anyone is in pain and sorrow, in the middle of human temptations, he may not imagine that because of that he is cut off from God's favour' (*in Ps.* 87.3). Christ not only identifies with humanity but identifies specially with those of weak will, tormented by fear; this is the point of the Gethsemane story (*in Ps.* 93.19). We believe Christ to have been wholly and perfectly at one with God the Father. If, then, he suffers fear and grief, this shows that these are not occasions for guilt, as if they were sins, but are the inevitable stuff of human experience in an alienated world (*in Ps.* 87.3), the objectified consequence (as for St Paul) of the 'wrath of God' (ibid. 7). Thus Christ's suffering has, so to speak, an exemplary quality: this, it says, is what the world is like, a world that crucifies its God, that crucifies compassion, that crucifies beauty. Yet to leave it at that would be wholly to ignore the reality of the Church as Christ's body; if we are *in* Christ, the relation between our suffering and his cannot simply be as 'external' as this. Christ said to Saul, 'Why persecutest thou *me*?' and this is 'the voice of the Head crying out on behalf of the Body' (*in Ps.* 55.3). 'Until the end of the world, if any member of My body is suffering, I suffer' (*in Ps.* 101.i.3). This is one of the most frequent and eloquently treated themes in the *Discourses on the Psalms* and should serve as a final rebuttal of the charge of moralism. The dereliction of Christ on the cross, where 'God cries out to God for mercy' (*in Ps.* 66.5), is repeatedly taken as the moment in which Christ shows himself paradigmatically human and gives voice to all human suffering, but especially to the sufferings of his Church, the body of those whose whole lives are lived under the sign of this strange *Deus crucifixus (Ps.* 93.15; and for the Head and Body theme, see *Ps.* 62.2, *Ps.* 68. i and ii, *passim P.s.* 87.14, *Ps.* 90, i and ii, *passim, Ps.* 9.3, *passim, Ps.* 123.1, *Ps.* 140.5–6, etc.; on Christ on the cross as Adam, see, e.g., *Ps.* 37.27). One of the most telling remarks in the *Discourses,* which would properly merit a detailed independent discussion, occurs in *in Ps.* 140.7: here Augustine says that the two texts which provide the key for the understanding of the whole of Scripture are the words to Paul on the Damascus road,'Why persecutest thou me?' and the parable of the Great Assize in Matthew 25 ('Inasmuch as ye have done it . . .'). In these sayings is affirmed the absolute unity of Christ with his suffering people; and this principle of God's identification with humanity is the clue to the whole of revelation. What is said of God in Christ can be applied to us, and what can be said of us in Christ can be applied to God. Christ suffers in our sufferings, *and* we in his – 'we too were there' (*in Ps.* 142.8). The pattern of Christ's cross is the meeting place of God and humanity. To become Godlike is to accept crucifixion by the destructiveness of the world.

There is, then, no route to God which does not pass under the cross, no exaltation without the prior humiliation known by Christ (*in Ps.* 119.1, *Ps.* 126.5). We advance 'from His pattern to His Godhead' (*in Ps.* 119.1). Augustine, again like Gregory of Nyssa, is intrigued by Moses' vision of God's 'back parts'; but for him this signifies the revelation of God in the humiliated and obscure life of Jesus. His divinity is hidden, and we grasp it purely by faith (*in Ps.* 120.6, *Ps.* 138.8ff,22). As for Ignatius, God is seen at work in darkness and in silence, declaring his mercy 'at night', in the middle of the world's chaos and wretchedness, under the world's ambiguous forms. Nearness to God and likeness to God are, as we have already noted, one and the same (*in Ps.* 94.2), and the cross is the model for our likeness to God (*in Ps.* 53.4, *Ps.* 93.15, *Ps.* 102.4, etc.). This is how God is known; in our weakness and fallenness we cannot comprehend what it is to share in God's life, but when we are set in the way of salvation, by penitence and humility, we do begin to know and understand (*in Ps.* 146.11,14). Augustine is not particularly fond of the familiar Greek language of 'deification' and prefers to use the scriptural terminology of adoptive sonship through baptism to make the point about participation in the divine life. 'When we are justified, we are made "gods", because we shall be called Sons of God' (*in Ps.* 49.2); and 'Out of sons of men He makes sons of God, because out of the Son of God He made a Son of Man . . . and in this is our promise of a share in divinity, (*in Ps.* 52.6; cf. *Ps.* 136.1). 'Deification' is conferred by the identification of the believer in baptism with the divine Son, whose own sonship is manifested in death and resurrection; it is not attained by a private flight of the soul to its divine source. Augustine was no less than truthful when he recorded in the *Confessions* that the point at which the gulf between Platonism and Christianity became most evident for him was the assertion that the eternal Logos became historical flesh (VII.9; cf.VII.18). And to know that requires the humility and the *caritas* which no philosophy can teach (ibid.VII.18,20).

Hope and Mystery

Augustine, more clearly than many other early Christian writers, presents a vision of the entirety of human experience caught up into grace and into God, of providence at work in sin, doubt, confusion, complex and imperfect motivation. A human life is given its unity and its intelligibility from outside: when God pulls taut the slack thread of desire, binding it to himself, the muddled and painful litter of experience is gathered together and given direction. This is implicit in Augustine's familiar account of the image of God in man. The threefold pattern in the human subject – intellect, memory and will – is the imprint *(vestigium)* of the causal acitivity of the Trinity, as are other triple structures (being, knowing and willing, for instance); it is not as such the *image* of God. The image is fulfilled when the *mens,* operating in *sapientia,* not *scientia,* 'tends' towards its prototype and becomes more than a mere 'analogy'. In this condition, the internal human 'trinity' is memory of God, understanding of God, and will or love directed to God (see, e.g., *de Trinitate* XV.20,39). The ordinary threefold analogy is activated and brought to full realization when the whole life of the *mens* turns to God. As J. E. Sullivan puts it in an important work on this aspect of Augustine's thought (*The Image of God: the Doctrine of St Augustine and Its Influence,* p. 147), 'it is only in knowing and loving God that the trinity in man becomes more and more like God.' The *mens* is Godlike in its making God its object. If its willing and loving are turned upon itself, it is infected with *amor potestatis suae,* love of its own power, which is inimical to God (*Ep.* 118.15); this is by no means the same as that *amor sui,* proper self-love, which the believer is enjoined to practise. 'Only he who loves God knows how to love himself' (*de mor.eccles.* 48); for without the love of God, we cannot know the self that is to be loved, and we live with delusory images of it. In God's light, the true self appears, in all its poverty and helplessness; yet it is lovable, because the breaking-in upon us of God's light is the evidence that *he* loves it. And what quarrel can there be with his love? Look at the cross, the great visible mark of God's compassion, and 'see how greatly He values you' (*in Ps.* 143.10).

God's love is entirely gratuitous, never a response to some innate beauty in *us.* 'In God there is the highest degree of loving kindness, holy and righteous, and this appears as love in all His doings – love, arising not from need, but from pure goodwill' (*de Genesi ad litteram* I. xi). We can accept our poverty and turn it to love because we are secure in the knowledge of being loved, being valued. The initiative is always God's, God's love breaking in with 'sweet violence' (*Serm.* 131.2) and irresistible force. 'No mortal man can escape the violence of death; and likewise the world can do nothing against the violence of love. . . . As death is most violent in taking away, so love is most violent in saving us' (*in Ps.* 47.13). Again, it is not hard to see how Augustine came to feel that the austere individualistic moralism of Pelagius and his followers was a mockery of the gospel. Where, in Pelagianism, was the sense of this 'violence' of God, the utterly gratuitous and unpredicted flow of mercy to his creatures, the sense of being grasped, overwhelmed and intoxicated? For one with Augustine's tortured past, with the experience of God accepting and transforming even the most tarnished and disorderly of lives, Pelagianism simply shut up the gate of heaven. And it is significant that it was the tenth book of the *Confessions* which first provoked Pelagius himself to indignation with Augustine; for what conclusion could be drawn by ordinary men and women from such a catalogue of weakness but that moral effort was useless? For the Pelagian, freedom was fundamental, the freedom to obey God's laws. For Augustine, as we have already seen, freedom is a far more ambivalent notion; in his more virulent works against Pelagius, he will come close to a total denial of freedom of choice both before and after the advent of grace. In the phrase that most deeply shocked Pelagius, Augustine can ask God to 'Give what You command, and command what You will' (*Conf.* x.29). Pelagius seeks freedom as the way by which salvation is attained; but for Augustine it is the issue, not the source, of salvation (*in Ps.* 83.1, *Ps.* 103.3, etc.). The Holy Spirit gives to the believer the fire of love (*in Ps.* 96.7), and freedom is nothing other than this love in the Holy Spirit. ' "I walked in liberty". What, then, do these words mean but "I walked in love"?' (*in Ps.* 118.xiv.2).

Between the worlds of Augustine and Pelagius – in the twentieth as much as in the fifth century – there can be little debate: the gulf is too wide. One person will see the world as difficult, but essentially capable of being 'tamed' – a challenge to the human faculties to exercise and extend themselves.

This will be a world in which heroism is possible, in which good causes can be believed in, improvement of self and others can be sought with a clear eye and a clean conscience. Guilt is a straightforward question of responsible and deliberate delinquency; virtue, of responsible and deliberate obedience. There is always a right answer. Iris Murdoch, writing of contemporary British moral philosophy, describes the inhabitant of this world with characteristic precision: '[His] merits are freedom (in the sense of detachment, rationality), responsibility, self-awareness, sincerity, and a lot of utilitarian common sense. There is of course no mention of sin, and no mention of love' (*The Sovereignty of Good*, p. 49; for a concrete portrayal of such a character, we may turn to the figure of James in her novel *The Bell*). In contrast, another will see the world as not merely difficult, but well-nigh intolerable, in no intelligible sense a challenge or an opportunity. This world represents sheer human defeat. In a sense it has no heroes: it has tragic protagonists, whose motivation is too unclear for them to be credibly heroic. Even its busiest agents are victims. Moral or social improvement is clouded by the certainty of failure and regression; and guilt and virtue are elusive and ambivalent ideas. Responsible and deliberate choice is the least part of motivation, good or ill. There are seldom right answers. Sin and love are categories of the first importance, two kinds of incalculable passionate forces. 'Sincerity' in the bland moralist's sense – a consciousness of one's own honesty – gives way to the despairing candour which recognizes that we do not *know* whether we are honest or not: there is too much in the psyche that is obscure for us ever to be confident of seeing or telling the truth about ourselves.

If the crude question is put which of these worlds is 'Christian', the answer is, neither. Neither despair nor bland assurance, but faith is the mark of the Christian. However, faith *does* depend upon an ability at least to 'entertain' the Augustinian picture, an ability to see the world as unclear and the human spirit as confused and imprisoned in fantasies. The Pelagian (or rationalist or positivist) sees no schism in the heart and so no need for healing reconciliation. If Paul's understanding of the cross of Jesus was and is correct, the need for reconciliation is a basic human datum; and if that is so, the Augustinian's world is less closed to the Gospel than the Pelagian's. The risk of irrationalism and quietism is great, and Augustinianism has been employed to justify many varieties of irresponsibility to which the Bishop of Hippo would have given no approval. Yet if Christianity does not have to do with – to be shamelessly emotive – love's mending of broken hearts, the risk is endemic and unavoidable. The world is a world capable of crucifying its own health, and the cross remains a stark reminder that there is little to hope for here. However, to concentrate exclusively on the dark side of Augustine's universe is misleading:there is little enough of hopefulness in the world, yet only in the world, only with other men and women, do we *learn* hope, pity, joy, trust or love. It is knowing both their utter and intense reality and their doomed frailty that begins to suggest to us the perspective of authentic hope.

To set Augustine beside the greatest of the Greek Christian writers is a curious and instructive exercise. Origen, Gregory and, later, Maximus the Confessor in the seventh century are all vividly conscious of the intellect's inadequacy, of the primacy of love, of the mysterious and intractable nature of human subjectivity; yet none of them sees all this in the tragic light which Augustine sheds upon it. One reason is that the Greeks tend to see salvation as almost wholly coterminous with liberation: grace makes us free to order our lives according to God's will. This is by no means a 'Pelagian' position (though sometimes referred to by the more or less meaningless term 'semi-Pelagian'), and it does not at all minimize the extent of conflict in the Christian life. Yet underlying all is a kind of optimism about human capacity which is absent from the mature work of Augustine. Evidently Augustine still thinks in terms of Christian vocation in the world (*The City of God* treats of precisely that); but the vocation is less to action than to faith. This is easily misinterpreted. As we have seen, Augustine never seeks to absolve the Christian from action. (He prays in his commentary *in Ps.* 118.x.3, 'Teach me so that I may *act*, not just know how I *ought* to act!) and allows the world's peace and justice to be desirable ends; but unless all is based on a recognition that action is formed by desire, by some fundamental direction or 'intentionality' of the self, frustration and disillusion (a different matter from 'unillusionedness') are inevitable. To be human is to desire, to be drawn and moulded by extra-rational, even extra-mental, attractive forces. Augustine's greatest legacy to Christian spirituality is the affirmation that the life of grace can include not only moral struggle and spiritual darkness, but also an awareness of the radically *conditioned* character of human behaviour – marked as we are in ways unknown to us by childhood experience, historical and social structures, and many more factors of which Augustine himself could not have been consciously aware, but to which our own age is especially sensitive. If human behaviour is such, the 'creation' of a life realizing the purposes of God, the transformation of image into likeness, is not impossible, but does take on a different quality. The emphasis must be not upon achievement but upon attitude. What holds a life together is simply the trust – or faith – that the eyes and the heart are turned towards truth, and that God accepts such a life without condition, looking on the will rather than *merely* the deed. God asks not for heroes but for lovers; not for moral athletes but for men and women aware of their need for acceptance, ready to find their selfhood in the longing for communion with an eternal 'other'.

This does not flatly contradict the 'Greek' model, but fleshes it out in a wider and darker human experience. Augustine, dying as the barbarians advanced towards his city, witnessing the collapse of a civilization in appalling human misery, is a long way from the still clear Hellenic light of Gregory. Peter Brown writes of Augustine's battle with Julian, 'Far above the sunlit surface of Julian's Bible, the God of Augustine had remained the ineffable God of the Neo-Platonic mystic' (*Augustine of Hippo,* p. 393). But the mystery of Augustine's God is not the static and solitary purity of Plotinus' 'One'; timeless and unchangeable as he is, Augustine's is rather the inscrutable God who speaks out of Job's whirlwind and makes himself known in a dying man – not 'far above', but penetrating every corner, mysterious with the tragic and terrifying mysteriousness of experience and history. 'Before experiencing God you thought you could talk about Him; when you begin to experience Him you realized that what you are experiencing you cannot put into words' (*in Ps.* 99.6). Gregory, or Plotinus himself, might have written that, but perhaps with more exhilaration and less pathos than does Augustine. It is not particularly surprising that Augustine was deeply, even disturbingly, affected by music, so much so that in *Conf.* X.33 he admits that he does not know how to manage his own response to music in church, oscillating between sheer emotional self-indulgence which concentrates on the beauties of sound at the expense of sense and purpose (the praise of God), and the puritanical closing of the ears which rejects one of the most potent means by which hearts are stirred to the love of God. What cannot be said may still be sung: sung not only in the hymns and psalms of which he is speaking in the *Confessions* passage, but in the wordless *jubilus*, the almost formless chant of the labourers in the fields:

> Singing to God properly is singing 'with jubilation' [*in jubilatione*]. Now what is this singing with jubilation? Think of people singing as they go about some hot and exhausting job – at harvest-time, say, or in the vineyard. They start celebrating in their happiness with the words of familiar songs. But they end up turning away from words and syllables, as if they were filled with so much happiness that they couldn't put it into words. And off they go into the noise of 'jubilation'. This kind of singing [*jubilum*] is a sound which means that the heart is giving birth to something it cannot speak of. And who better to receive such 'jubilation' than the ineffable God – ineffable, because you cannot talk about Him. And if you cannot talk about Him, and it is improper just to keep silence, why, what is there left for you to do but 'jubilate' – with your heart rejoicing without words, and the immense breadth of your joy not rationed out in syllables? (*in Ps.* 32.8).

> So when do we 'jubilate'? When we praise what we cannot speak of (*in Ps.* 99.5).

There is one of Augustine's most memorable images of Christian prayer and praise. But more profound and suggestive is another image drawn from music, occurring in the last few pages of the *Discourses on the Psalms,* expressing so much of his teaching on grace, desire, purification from the world's ways, and the sheer beauty of truth that it might well serve as a summary of his vision. He is commenting on the words, 'Let them sing praises unto him with tabret and harp' (*Ps.* 149.3):

> We should not pass over the mysterious meaning of 'tabret and harp' in silence. On a tambourine you have a skin stretched out, and in a stringed instrument you have catgut stretched out. So in both instruments ordinary flesh is being 'crucified'. The man who said, 'The world is crucified to me and I to the world' (Gal.6.14) must have sung praises really well on this 'tabret and harp'! And He Who loves a 'new song' wants to take you to be that harp, that tabret. He gives you His instructions when He says, 'Whoever wants to be my disciple, let him deny himself and take up his cross and follow me'. Do not let Him throw away His harp and His tabret. Let them be stretched out on the wood [of the cross], and all fleshly desire dried out of them. Strings or sinews [*nervi*] sound more sharply the more they are stretched out. And what does Paul the apostle say about making his harp sound more sharp and clear? 'Forgetting what lies behind and straining forward (*extentus*) to what lies ahead, I press on toward the goal for the prize of the upward call' (Phil. 3.13,14). So he stretched himself out; Christ touched him, and the sweetness of truth gave tongue (*in Ps.* 149.8).

This passage must have been in George Herbert's mind when, more than a thousand years later, he wrote:

> Awake, my lute, and struggle for thy part
>   With all thy art.
> The crosse taught all wood to resound his name,
>   Who bore the same.
> His stretched sinews taught all strings, what key
> Is best to celebrate this most high day.
>   (*Easter,* v.2).

The violent love of God breaks through deafness and blindness; the violent desire of human souls for God breaks through dumbness. The heart has no words, but it cannot contain itself in silence: 'Love grown cold is the heart's silence; love on fire, the heart's clamour' (*in Ps.* 36.14).

5. Acrobats and Jugglers

The City

Technically, Augustine lived in a Christian Empire. The Christian religion had been made fully legal by Constantine in 313, and Theodosius had made it the official creed of the *imperium Romanum* in 389. Yet Augustine in *The City of God* treats the Empire as doomed, and justly so, as a 'city' built on violence and oppression whose long-deserved nemesis has at last come. For Rome had fallen to the Goths in 410, and Augustine was writing to those who regarded this as a catastrophe for the Church. In the massive perspective of *The City of God,* the fall of the city becomes one more in the catalogue of human tragedies in the midst of which the Church always stands – 'The most glorious city of God, both as it lives by faith in the course of these days, a pilgrim among the wicked, and as it exists in the stability of the eternal resting place for which it now waits in patience' (*de civ. Dei* I.*Praef.*). Whatever the social order, the Church is still on pilgrimage; and the 'Christian Empire' is as transitory and ambiguous a phenomenon as any other social form. Augustine lived to see the near-total collapse of Roman authority in the province of Africa; he died as the barbarians began the siege of Hippo. To him, as to most sensitive Christians in Africa and Western Europe, any notion of the Empire as a sacral kingdom under divine protection would have been painfully absurd.

Constantine, however, had sought to give solid expression

to the renewal of the Empire under the protection of the Christian God by the building of a Christian city, a Christian New Rome, on the shores of the Bosphorus, at Byzantium. And for the Greek section of the Empire, the existence of Constantinople as a Christian Rome, housing the court of a Christian ruler, had the force of an eschatological sign, a portent of the Last Days, of the imminence of the Kingdom. Constantine's most devoted eulogist, Eusebius of Caesarea, can speak of the Christian Kingdom as an image, an *eikon,* of the heavenly Kingdom, with the Emperor as the image of the Logos from whom the universe draws its ordered and rational structure (see the *Oration in Honour of Constantine on the Thirtieth Anniversary of his Reign,* 1–3). For those who thought in this way, the fall of Old Rome hardly mattered; in the East it was left to Latin exiles such as Jerome to lament the tragedy. The pressure for the Church to detach itself from the secular locations of authority, which bore so heavily on Augustine, was hardly sensed. Once, and only very recently in the Eastern Empire, persecution had made a 'long divorce of steel' between Church and *imperium:* the martyr was the clear sign of the conflict between the two cities. Now, in the West, the Church was compelled to deny that its survival or its identity depended upon the survival of Rome and *Romanitas,* and to begin the long and weary task of making some accommodation with the barbarians. But in the East the elect prince now ruled over the people of God, and the good of the Church and the good of the City were not for many centuries to be so rudely forced apart. Life in the City, under the king, the *basileus,* was God's ordinance in making humanity fit for his eternal *basileia.*

The protest was to come from one of the least sophisticated areas of Eastern Roman society, the peasantry of Egypt and Syria. They were those who, in any case, had least investment in the Christian *basileia,* geographically and socially marginal, people for whom the ideology of the administration made little difference to its effect upon them. The emperor and his administration might be an icon of the court of heaven, but for the peasant they could not be other than a remote despotism responsible for ever more ruinous taxation. The peasant was not a citizen but merely a subject of the

City; to identify the Christian life with 'life in the City' was as meaningless as it was to become later in the West when there was no City. Thus the flight from the City, the deliberate isolation of oneself from the social order, from family and civic life and financial transaction, is a statement of the belief that Christian possibilities cannot be exhausted by life in the City. Before the state had been nominally christianized, the fact of martyrdom had made this all too obvious: the destiny of Christian life might well be that most uncompromising refusal of the City which the martyr pronounced. Under a baptized emperor, there might be no martyrs; but this fact would be liable to obscure the abiding truth that claims of the City and those of God were not coterminous. And it is in this sense that it has been rightly said that monasticism is a kind of substitute for martyrdom: a less dramatic but no less serious witness to the tension between this age and the age to come, to the *absence* of the Kingdom of God on earth. Karl Barth, no uncritical devotee of monasticism, allows that 'the way into the desert', so far from being an escape, may be seen as 'a highly responsible and effective protest and opposition to the world, and not least to a worldly Church, a new and specific way of combating it, and therefore a direct address to it' (*Church Dogmatics* IV.2, p. 13). It is a challenge to the Church to beware of defining itself too narrowly, a rejection of any kind of 'culture-religion'. And as such it always risks a measure of absurdity, or at least incongruity, in the eyes of the world and of the worldly Church.

Antony, the founding father of the monastic movement, is alleged to have said: 'A time is coming when men will go mad, and when they see someone who is not mad, they will attack him saying, "You are mad, you are not like us" ' (*The Sayings of the Desert Fathers. The Alphabetical Collection*, tr. Benedicta Ward, SLG, p. 5). As a statement of the intractable oddity of monasticism, that cannot be improved upon. The world and the Church are mad when they circumscribe human possibilities of serving God; it is left for the ironic sanity of the monk or nun to demonstrate – at some personal cost – that God's call is a far stranger thing than any human social definitions might allow. Antony himself sold his goods and began his new life in the mid-third century, long before the Constantinian 'conversion of Christianity' (in Peter Brown's phrase). He was (as his biographer, the great Athanasius, makes clear) not the first Christian solitary in the Egyptian desert; what seems to have given him a unique position was the fact that his emergence (in *c*.305) from complete solitude to act as spiritual father to the recluses who had settled near him coincided with the early period of the Arian crisis. He and his followers cast their considerable moral weight on the Athanasian side; and when, after Constantine's death, imperial authority – the authority of the City – supported Arianism, the cleft between God and the City appeared in full clarity to many in the Catholic party. Antony himself survived to the age of one hundred and five, dying in about 356, and so remained a powerful personal focus for the monastic protest when this was most needed. Thanks to his championship of Athanasius, monasticism was established by the mid-fourth century as a sign to the orthodox of the Church's essential freedom from even a professedly Christian state; of the Church's right to declare its own self-interpretation, even if the City disagreed. It was an ambiguous heritage, as it turned out: the militancy, even brutality, of monastic doctrinal protest in the following century is disgraceful and shocking. But monasticism was to remain as a hint to the Byzantine world and its satellites that the Last Day had still to come; it saved the Christian East from total domination by the graceless theocratic ideology of a Eusebius.

The Desert

Antony would have thought of none of these things. His original protest was a local and personal matter. In about 269, aged eighteen or nineteen, he heard read at the Eucharist in his rural Egyptian church the Lord's injunction to 'sell what you possess and give to the poor'. There was no Clement of Alexandria at hand to explain that this has a primarily interior and spiritual sense: Antony, by the grace of God, was an unenlightened literalist. He promptly distributed the inheritance left him at the death of his parents 'which had occurred shortly before this event'), and began to lead a life of 'discipline', *askesis.* For many years he simply lived in prayer and poverty among his village neighbours, under the direction of an older man living a similar life of retirement nearby. Not until *c.* 285 did he withdraw completely to the desert. This pattern of 'disciplined' life in the middle of the community was not uncommon in Egypt and Syria around this time; it is only very gradually that the sense of a 'new thing' grows – a combination of the unusual insight and attractiveness of Antony himself, and of his decision to involve the monastic witness in the life of the wider Church by taking sides in the Arian crisis. 'Monasticism' was to become something distinct from the simple pattern of 'discipline' followed unobtrusively by isolated men and women scattered here and there in Mediterranean town and villages.

The monastic objection was to a Christian life deprived of its tension towards the future, the *eschaton;* so it is not surprising to find the theme of growth-through-conflict enjoying great prominence in the early monastic world. Nowhere is there any suggestion that the monastic profession in itself achieves anything: its purpose is to provide a stable geographical and psychological location where the important battles may be fought. For many of the earliest monks, stability of place was the primary condition for all else – 'Stay in your cell, and your cell will teach you everything.' 'Let your imagination think what it likes, only do not let your body leave the cell' (*The Wisdom of the Desert Fathers. Apophthegmata Patrum (The Anonymous Series),* tr. Benedicta Ward, SLG, p. 24). What is useless and destructive is to imagine that enlightenment or virtue can be found by seeking for fresh stimulation. The monastic life is a refusal of any view that will make human maturity before God dependent on external stimulus, 'good thoughts', good impressions, edifying influences and ideas. Instead, the monk must learn to live with his own darkness, with the interior horror of temptation and fantasy. Salvation affects the whole of the psyche; to try to escape boredom, sexual frustration, restlessness, unsatisfied desire by searching for fresh tasks and fresh ideas is to attempt to seal off these areas from grace. Without the humiliating and wholly 'unspiritual' experiences of cell-life – the limited routine of trivial tasks, the sheer tedium and loneliness – there would be no way of confronting much of human nature. It is a discipline to destroy illusions. The monk has come to the desert to escape the illusory Christian identity proposed by the world; he now has to see the roots of illusion in himself, in his longing to be dramatically and satisfyingly in control of his life, the old familiar imperialism of the self bolstered by the intellect.

That is why Antony firmly states that everyone must 'expect temptation to his last breath' and that 'Whoever has not experienced temptation cannot enter into the Kingdom of Heaven' (*The Sayings of the Desert Fathers,* p. 2). And there are cautionary tales of those who fondly imagined that they had eradicated their propensity to selfishness and evil – the smug old man whom Abba Abraham forced to admit that the passions were still active in him, controlled but not destroyed (ibid., p. 29), and others whose self-discovery was more painful and eventful. A pointed little story is told of Abba John the Dwarf, who prayed to be delivered from the passions and, rather surprisingly, was. But when he confided this happy result to a senior brother, he was told, in effect, to ask God to give them back to him, 'so that you may regain the affliction and humility that you used to have, for it is by warfare that the soul makes progress'. The right prayer is for strength, not deliverance (ibid., p. 75). The quality of Christian life is unease, battle – not the unease of the heart, as for Augustine, but the ceaseless engagement of the will. And there is clearly in this attitude a very problematic element indeed. The positive side of it is a realistic acknowledgement of conflict as the means of growth, and of the inevitability of boredom, fantasy, and so on; it is a warning against complacency, against a static and self-oriented spiritual life. The negative side is an emphasis on effort and vigilance (literally), sleepless alertness, which often seems simply neurotic and lays itself open to that romanticism of the will which Augustine turned from so violently – a spirituality of the super-ego.

There is no resolution of this; even at the beginnings of monasticism it is possible to see what the Reformers were to object to, an apparent glorification of will at the expense of grace. Yet, finally, primitive monasticism is on the side of grace, if only because of the profound acceptance of *failure* in so many of the Desert Fathers. Macarius the Great, one of the most attractive figures of the early days of desert monasticism, gave to one brother the sound advice that 'if an alien thought arises' he should 'never look at it but always look upwards'. Macarius had brought this man to an admission of his tormented condition simply by speaking to him of his own, Macarius', troubles (*Sayings*, p. 107); and here we touch on one of the deepest realities in the life of the desert, the reluctance to pass judgement on another and the ability of the great 'old men' to identify unreservedly with the uncertainties and suffering of others. 'They said of Abba Macarius that he became, as it is written, a god upon earth, because, just as God protects the world, so Abba Macarius would cover the faults which he saw, as though he did not see them; and those which he heard, as though he did not hear them' (ibid., p. 113). And there are the numerous stories describing how an innocent brother would share the penance of a sinful monk (see, for example, *Wisdom*, pp. 15, no. 47, and 36, no. 123): 'See what it is', says the compiler of the *Anonymous Series* of sayings, 'to give one's soul for one's brother' (ibid., p. 15). The uncomprising summons to the will to stir itself is balanced by the recognition that the will's failure is not everything, that forgiveness is possible, and that the love of the brethren will continue to support the sinner. For all the emphasis on 'fleeing from men', solitude and silence, the love of neighbour remains fundamental: 'Abba John the Dwarf said, "A house is not built by beginning at the top and working down. You must begin with the foundations. . . . The foundation is our neighbour whom we must win. . . . For all the commandments of Christ depend on this one" ' (*Sayings*, pp. 79–80). In one of the letters attributed to Antony (no. 6; tr. D. Chitty, *The Letters of St Antony the Great*, p. 20), we read that 'He who sins against his brother sins against himself'; and in the *Life* (para. 67), Antony is represented as saying, 'If we gain our brother, we gain God'. It is interesting that, in the same sixth letter, the writer describes heaven as a state in which we shall see each other face to face (ed. cit., p. 23). This recalls not only Augustine's 'night of the world', when human hearts are hidden from each other, but one of the stories told of Macarius, who is informed by the spirit of a dead pagan priest that in hell 'it is not possible to see anyone face to face, but the face of one is fixed to the back of another. Yet when you pray for us, each of us can see the other's face a little' (*Sayings,* p. 115).

Thus when Abba Moses instructs Abba Poemen that 'The monk must die to his neighbour and never judge him at all, in any way whatever' (ibid., p. 119), we see the essential significance of the image of death in the monastic mind. Moses continues by saying that the monk 'must die to everything . . . *in order not to harm anyone'* (ibid.; my italics). 'Death' is withdrawal from the possibility of imposing the violence of selfishness on others; it is allowing the freedom and the separateness of the other to flourish unhindered. If you have a dead body in your home, said Moses, you do not go to weep for a neighbour's bereavement (ibid., p. 120); so weep for your sins, which you know, not for your neighbour's, which you do not know. As Abba John the Dwarf said, the vocation of each saint is distinctive – different trees watered from one source (ibid., p. 81); no one can assess the adequacy of a brother's way of life. The visitor who was surprised at the difference between the austere and silent Arsenius and the cheerful, welcoming Moses was shown a vision which made it clear that both were as they were for God's sake: 'Two large boats were shown him on a river and he saw Abba Arsenius and the Spirit of God sailing in the one, in perfect peace; and in the other was Abba Moses with the angels of God, and they were all eating honey cakes' (ibid., p. 15). Another visitor, shocked that Arsenius was allowed some small extra comforts, was reminded that the old man had been an imperial counsellor, living in luxury utterly unknown to the peasants who made up the majority of the monks; they – including the critic – were often more comfortable than they had been in the world (ibid., p. 14). But perhaps the most impressive story is that told of Antony himself, and subsequently of many others: God reveals to the monk that he has a spiritual equal in the city, an ordinary layman of some kind (in Antony's case, a doctor), living no less in sacrificial poverty and humility (see, e.g., *Sayings,* p. 5).

Primitive monasticism is a search for a context in which

illusions and distortions of reality can be removed – individual reality, the reality of other persons, social reality. Growth cannot occur without the stripping of illusion; and the great contribution of monasticism to Christianity (as, in different but related ways, in oriental religions) is the acknowledgement that the believing community as a whole can save itself from seduction and deceit only if it allows for some who are prepared to undertake a drastic surgery upon the fantasizing and dominating self, and so remind the whole Body of its vulnerability, its liability to live at a level of unseriousness. And it becomes increasingly clear, from Antony onwards, that such a surgery needs to be performed with at least a measure of assistance and mutual support in community, where each is obliged to learn to let the other exist in his own space, not conforming to egocentric projection or to standardized expectations of 'spirituality'. And this again is balanced by a stress on obedience to the 'old men', especially to the single 'elder' or spiritual father under whose direction the young monk lives. The community allows for many styles of life, but it does not become a random collection of eccentrics because there is so constant a stress upon obedience, being formed by *attending* to others. Each ascetic is allowed his freedom, his distance, from the others; he is not moulded by an imposed general discipline; yet he is to find his vocation in and only in attention to the brethren and obedience to the elders. Even the most solitary of ascetics must begin with the brethren, sharing their trials as they share his, without judging or dominating. It is a subtle and difficult balance, not easily maintained; and given the eccentricities of some ascetic individualists – especially in Syria and Asia Minor – it is not surprising that more attention soon came to be given to corporate organization and structure. Pachomius in Egypt between 320 and 346 established a strict communal order for his monks at Tabennisis; and later in the century the great Basil of Caesarea performed the same service for monasticism in Asia Minor, with the two collections of instructions rather misleadingly called the 'Longer Rules' and 'Shorter Rules' (they are not 'Rules' in the later sense of a systematic programme for monastic life, as their 'question and answer' form clearly shows). The corporate institutional forms deriving from Pachomian and Basilian monasticism were to provide a norm for male and female religious life which still largely determines the patterns of monasticism today. Side by side with the desert tradition, they provide a 'classical' point of reference.

So it is far too facile to see in this development the triumph of the 'institutional' over the 'charismatic'. Basil's concern, as the 'Rules' make clear, is to make sure that liberty does not become self-indulgence. The decrees of the Synod of Gangra (340) show how far some kinds of monastic eccentricity had gone and how much there had grown up in some areas an arrogant sense of the monk's superiority to the Church at large. Gangra particularly condemns those who claim that the monastic state is superior to the married, and those who hold aloof from the Eucharist, preferring private piety to the activity of the whole Body of Christ. It is against this background that Basil writes; and it is not hard to understand his scepticism about the glories of the solitary life. None of us is materially self-sufficient: 'God the Creator arranged things so that we need each other' (*Longer Rules* VII). And, more importantly, the two essentials of Christian (and so of monastic) life, growth in love and growth in humility, cannot be realized in solitude. Someone will have to guide and rebuke you; someone should be there to receive your service. If you live alone, 'whose feet are you going to wash?' How will you learn patience without the irritation of having people around resisting you or disagreeing with you? And all this comes finally to two basic theological data: the incarnation and the existence of the Body of Christ on earth. Christ came to serve in self-forgetfulness; how can he be imitated by the solitary? The Church is a harmony of diverse persons serving not their own needs but each others', sharing individual gifts with all; how can a person live *in the Church* as a solitary (ibid)? The brother who neglects 'any spiritual or physical needs' of his neighbour is guilty of *philautia*, self-love (*Shorter Rules* LIV): insensitivity of this kind is the mark by which the lover of self is known. And plainly Basil regards the solitary as more liable than most to this. Whether or not he envisaged as legitimate the possibility of withdrawal to solitude after some time spent in the common life is not at all clear. Such an allowance on his part could not have been at all enthusiastic, since the whole of his theology of the monastic life is dependent to a rare degree on the incarnate life of Christ as a model; it would be virtually impossible for him to have produced a convincing theology for hermits.

The *horos* – the standard or definition – of Christian life is 'the imitation of Christ according to the extent [or 'measure'] of His incarnation' (*Longer Rules* XLIII). Basil comes back repeatedly to this theme: Christ is the servant of all in his earthly life, and nothing less is demanded of us. In a short treatise 'On Renouncing the World' (*de renuntiatione saeculi* 211C), he says quite simply that 'humility is the imitation of Christ'. And this includes a readiness to sacrifice our lives, our whole selves, for righteous and sinners alike, since Christ loves all alike and dies for all alike (*Shorter Rules* CLXXXVI). Everyone has equal claim on the Christian's unconditional service, because of the unconditional self-offering of Christ to all. Grace is free to everyone, and so must be the love and practical compassion of the believer; we may recall Basil's indefatigable energy and ability as a social reformer, the schools, hospitals and orphanages which sprang up in such abundance around his episcopal seat. And, of course, the theme of Christ's humility and service leads to some searching reflections on the role of the superior in a community. For Basil (as for Pachomius) the authority of an elected leader has replaced the authority of the charismatic elder – necessarily so, in a larger and more complex monastic society; but Basil, while allowing the superior an enormous scope for the exercise of his authority, opens his detailed discussion of the superior's office by insisting upon the primacy of Christlike service. Christian authority inverts the world's order, because 'the Lord was not ashamed to wait on His own slaves' (*Longer Rules* XLIII). The superior, indeed, has to practise a kind of 'obedience' to the community, in that it is his responsibility to adapt his guidance and leadership to the needs of each individual brother: he has to 'attend' to them as they attend to him. It becomes his charge, in fact, to ensure that the community does not crush the individual, that the liberty and spaciousness of desert monasticism survive in the institution. He shares in the availability and the painstaking, *exact* compassion of Christ; it is for him to show to the brethren the pattern of Christlikeness which they too must realize.

The Monastery

The traditions of Eastern monasticism travelled westwards by many routes; but one of the most important 'carriers' was the work of Cassian (360–435), a Scythian who had lived with the 'old men' in Egypt and Syria and ended his life in Gaul, founding two communities near Marseilles. In the early 420s, he made a digest of the teaching of the great leaders of the desert in two books, the *Institutes* and the *Conferences (Collationes),* works which were to become the staple diet of Western monks and nuns until the Counter-Reformation. The *Conferences* in particular, composed in the form of discourses by the great abbas to their disciples were – in the words of Dom David Knowles – 'a classic without rival in the monastic west' (*Christian Monasticism,* p. 15). Cassian had been deeply influenced by the writings of Evagrius, and the discourses of the fathers are evidently cast in an artificial form characterized by an Evagrian vocabulary with which the Egyptian monks of the first generation would have been neither familiar nor sympathetic. There is much stress on the escape from 'mobility' of soul into stability and purity (see *Coll.* VII, *passim*), 'imperturbable peace' and 'uninterrupted prayer' (ibid. IX.2), the *nous* flying home to God. But this is side by side with a clear Christocentrism and an equal stress on charity as the image of God (ibid. I. 6–7, XI.9), and the forgiveness of enemies as a particularly God-like act (ibid. XV.10). Both the *Institutes* (IV.39) and the *Conferences* (XV.7, XVIII.13,ii) have the beginnings of what was to become a regular feature of monastic literature, a discussion of the grades and kinds of humility, the 'queen of virtues' (*Coll.* XV.7). So the potential individualism and even esotericism of Evagrian spirituality is countered by the characteristic monastic appeal to the model of Christ the merciful, Christ the servant. Cassian, like Evagrius, actively discourages meditation on the historical Christ; yet this cannot be taken (any more than it can in Origen's case) to deny the centrality of the role and status of Christ. Cassian can describe the Christian life in terms of the 'spirit of adoption' (*Coll.* XI,9, XXIV.26.iv) and of sharing in the love and the life of the Trinity (ibid. X.7), and here he is most clearly the heir of the biblical and relational aspects of Origenism. Nor can one ever forget in reading him that he is writing about *communal* life. Fergus Kerr, OP, has said of Cassian that he 'presupposes . . . that we cannot tackle the problem of how to pray without first facing the problem of our bad or poor relationships with other people'. ('Prayer and Community' in *Religious Life Today,* by John Coventry, SJ, Abbot Rembert Weakland, OSB and others, p. 39). It is made clear that the life of growth towards Christ as saviour and servant is possible only in the context of humanly directed charity and compassion – the corporate life of humility and patience.

Benedict (*c.*480 – *c.*547) incorporates the insight of both Basil and Cassian in one of the most remarkable documents of monastic history. The *Rule for Monks* is a comparatively brief, practical (almost prosaic) work, a 'little rule for beginners' (ch.73), yet its influence on the whole course of Western civilization has been vast. It is lucid, moderate, pithy and realistic, pervaded by a simple incarnational theology: a work, in fact, of rare genius. One notable feature is the prevalence of military imagery – none too surprising, perhaps, in the turbulent fifth century in Italy. The monk is addressed in the Prologue as one who is 'putting aside [his] own will so as to go to war under Christ the Lord, the real King, picking up the keen and glittering weapons of obedience'; and he is described a little later (ch.1) as *militans,* 'doing military service, under a rule and an abbot'. It is a powerful reminder of the primacy of obedience in monastic life; yet, as in Basil, it is qualified by a concern for the manner in which authority is exercised and for the overall purpose of the life of obedience – the renunciation of self-will in order to live accordng to the pattern of Christ. The abbot 'is believed to hold Christ's place in the monastery', and his name is based on the 'Abba' which believers address to God; he must teach by 'what he does even more than by what he says'; he must love all equally and adapt himself to each one's needs (ch.2), consulting the whole community when any significant decision has to be taken (ch.3). So the abbot, in his humility and respect for all, sets the standard for the whole community. All should be characterized by reverence for each other (ch.4.8, 30–2, 64–70, ch.63, ch.71, etc.); but in particular the sick in the community (ch.36) and guests, especially the poor (ch.53), are to be treated as Christ (rich guests, as Benedict sarcastically remarks, can rely on the awe they inspire to win them respect).

It is clearly stated in the Prologue that monasticism involves sharing in the sufferings of Christ, and chapter 5, 'On Obedience', relates monastic obedience to Christ's saying, 'I have come not to do my own will.' The Rule epitomizes the monastic rationale: here are persons attempting to create, by grace, the likeness of Christ, forming themselves and each other in a shared life. The enterprise of Christian growth towards the selfless service which God himself performs for men is seen as intimately bound up with a pattern of life together – not only in the wider community of the Church, but also in a tighter, more consciously 'therapeutic' group (such as the earliest Christian communities were in any case). To quote Fergus Kerr again, 'Relationship with others is the *form* that our growth in virtue takes: it is more than merely the *occasion*' (op. cit., p. 43). The whole of early monastic literature assumes that the kind of maturation of which Origen or Gregory of Nyssa speaks is not possible without the challenge of realizing 'virtue' in dealings with the concrete, resistant reality of another human being. The process of growth cannot be unequivocally internalized; yet again we are reminded how little Christianity is a religion of 'private experience'. Augustine himself had gathered to him a group of colleagues and friends to live 'under rule', to discover their Christian character in a shared discipline; and he understood so fully the part played by human friendship (and un-friendship) in the life of grace. But the more radical monasticism of the desert, and the great legislators, approached the human problem at one level even more pessimistically than did Augustine. The shared life *must* be a withdrawn life; there are some social contexts in which the only victory is retreat, which so cloud the face of reality that the only way to 'unillusionedness' is flight. And it must be life under obedience: the eradiction of self-will is so fundamentally important that the most stringent measures will be justified in effecting it. Christ's self-abandonment culminates in the cross; and it is a regular practice, especially in Eastern Christian art, to portray the monk as crucified. The comparison with martyrdom is seriously meant.

There remains the Augustinian problem about the will. Cassian was to draw upon himself the hostility of Augustine's followers by his advocacy (in *Coll.* XIII) of what came to be called 'synergism' – the model of co-operation between God's will and activity and human will and activity. The Augustinian could only regard this as naive, an inheritance from the blandest kind of Hellenistic optimism. To exert the will strenuously in order to destroy the power of *self*-will looks to be a rather self-defeating exercise, and to speak of 'co-operation' between human beings and God, as if each had some clearly demarcated sphere of action and power, is absurd. And it must be granted, I believe, that a good deal of ascetical literature does operate with some such naive view – as we have remarked above; the heritage of Stoic exaltation of the will dies hard, even now. Yet Benedict, following the fathers of the desert, assumes throughout the Rule that weakness and failure are the common order of monastic life (there is a moving allusion in chapter 27 to the parable of the Good Shepherd); and in his enumeration of the 'instruments of good works' (ch.4), he gives a place to the very Augustinian characteristics of 'desiring everlasting life with all the passion of the spirit' and 'never despairing of God's mercy'. Benedict's monks are not heroes of the will nor, in that deeply ambiguous phrase so beloved of spiritual writers, 'athletes of the spirit'. They persevere by grace, in hope and desire. And, more importantly still, the whole monastic emphasis on *attention* to the brethren serves to reduce the emphasis on the self and its solitary battles and direct us to the importance of learning how to *respond*. The Augustinian soul moves among massed psychological forces, and its task is simply to find the stream which can carry it home; in his last years, Augustine more and more considered the soul to be from the beginning in one stream or another and practically incapable of moving itself.

But this does mean, among other things, that the soul can move only when it is moved; the ego is not an unmoved mover, but is touched and drawn. And the monastic insight is to recognize how much of this moving and drawing is mediated in human community, how much the barriers of egotistic fantasy are broken by the sheer brute presence of other persons. The will 'co-operates' precisely because it is limited and constrained, attracted or repelled, irritated and tantalized by the boundaries set by others around it. God is to be apprehended under the form of those boundaries. As has often been said, the vow of obedience 'objectifies providence'. The superior, the sick brother, the guest, the pauper are, for the monk, Christ's face turned towards him, claiming and drawing: the face he must learn to reflect. There is simply no leisure to think about heroism.

Bernard of Clairvaux (1090–1153)

Throughout the 'Dark Ages', Benedict's rule dominated the Western monastic world. But it is misleading to think of European monasteries in these centuries as being populated by 'Benedictine monks', as if 'Benedictinism' were a clear, homogeneous phenomenon. David Knowles, in his major work on *The Monastic Order in England* (especially pp. 18 ff), has explained how the *Rule* functioned as a general guide rather than a 'constitution' in a wide variety of monasteries, whose practices resembled each other as little as they resembled the original pattern of Benedict's own community. The work of scholarship and the solemn performance of the liturgy were two things which the Middle Ages, and the Benedictine 'revivalists' of the nineteenth century, believed to be typically Benedictine activities. Yet the former derived not from Benedict but from Cassiodorus, a younger contemporary, who founded the first monastery to be self-consciously a centre of learning (at Vivarium in Calabria, in 540); and the latter reflects the practice of the great 'basilican' monasteries in Rome, the communities which sustained the regular worship of the major Roman churches. More and more communities of both sorts adopted the *Rule* in the sixth and seventh centuries; but they treated it as something to be used in conjunction with the tradition of the particular monastery. Like Basil's 'Rules' in the East, it was a spiritual rather than a legislative programme. Some kind of uniformity emerged by the early ninth century, with the work of Benedict of Aniane, whose reforms were imposed by law throughout the empire of Charlemagne – reforms which had the general effect of making 'Benedictinism' far more closely associated with the 'basilican' style of monasticism, concerned primarily with liturgy. But this uniformity has little to do with an imposition of strict observance of the *Rule.* St Benedict had not envisaged anything like the increasingly lengthy ceremonial programme of the ninth-century communities or its apotheosis at the great abbey of Cluny in Burgundy, in the tenth and eleventh centuries. Practice was established by a combination of *Rule* and custom.

The same flexibility with regard to the *Rule* appears in the radical monastic reformers of the eleventh and early twelfth century – Romuald, Peter Damian, Stephen of Muret and others. Their concern, however, is not to modify the *Rule,* but to go behind it to the primitive realities of the desert, even appealing (in Damian's case) to the example of Elijah. They accept Benedict's statement that the *Rule* does not establish 'the full observance of righteousness' and consciously attempt to deal with the stage 'beyond' the *Rule,* envisaging greater silence and solitude and intensity of prayer. For Damian there was also the element of restoring to the monastic movement its original character as a *protest,* against both the corruption of the Church at large and some of the reforming methods and measures of Pope Gregory VII in the mid-eleventh century. His attitude to Gregory's reforms was complex: he was a savage castigator of lax clerical morals, yet evidently felt that the kind of authority George was seeking to establish in the Church was dangerously secular in character, coercive and violent. Again, monastic radicalism addresses not only the world but the worldly Church – this time a Church never more worldly than when it seeks a sharply defined and tightly controlled identity over against a parallel system of 'worldly' government. But Stephen of

Muret is perhaps the most odd and original reformer of this period, refusing at first to give his hermit brethren any rule other than 'the Gospel, which is the chief of all rules' (Migne, PL 204, col. 1024). Although he eventually produced a rule of sorts, he gave great cause for puzzlement to his contemporaries by refusing to identify his style of monastic observance with any familiar model, insisting always on the simple call to imitate the poverty and humility of Christ.

It was the Cistercian reform, beginning at the very end of the eleventh century and coming to flower in the first half of the twelfth, that was to insist on exact observance of the *Rule, ad apicem litterae* ('to the last detail of the letter'), and treat it as a constitution or a lawbook. Paradoxically, the result was to produce a form of life no less remote (in many ways) from Benedict's communities than were the Cluniac houses. But at the time the Cistercian movement had an importantly liberating effect, freeing the monk from being simply a professional 'liturgist' and restoring something of the simplicity of the earliest days. One difference, though, was that manual labour was now shared between choir-monks and a huge population of *conversi,* illiterate lay-brothers who were chiefly responsible for much of the great labour of clearing and reclaiming land for farming, in which the Cistercians rapidly became expert and successful. The quite phenomenal spread of Cistercian monasticism in the twelfth century has much to do with its accessibility to the uneducated, to whom it offered an authentically monastic life without the labour of a long and difficult training for the priesthood. But it also has to do with the climate of ecclesiastical life at the time, a climate greatly preoccupied with the question of limits, definitions and laws, with securing the position of the Western Church as a kind of parallel state, with its own jurisprudence, administered by professional canon lawyers, and its own supreme court and chief magistrate in the Roman Curia and the Pope. It was a moment when the advantage would lie with a style of monasticism that could point to a clear charter, a clear set of prescriptions, a clear identity.

But all this might still not have added up to such a massive flood of men into the Cistercian order without the genius of one extraordinary man, who joined the movement at a point when its future was still rather uncertain: Bernard of Clairvaux (1090–1153), in his lifetime one of the most powerful men in Europe. Bernard is a maddeningly paradoxical man: intolerant and unjust, sometimes politically unscrupulous, with an astonishing confidence in his own authority, and yet also loving and compassionate, reconciling, humble, bitterly aware of the oddity of his own position as a monk wielding vast influence in the world. He inspired more deep love than hate and, for all his passionate and partisan involvement in controversies of all sorts, left few real enemies. And as a pastor to his own flock at Clairvaux he appears in his most attractive light, as poet, contemplative and teacher. Although the great series of sermons on the Song of Songs was probably not delivered as it stands to his monks (see Dom Jean Leclercq's introduction to volume III of *The Works of Bernard of Clairvaux* in the new Cistercian Publications translation), the style of his verbal teaching is clearly discernible here; to read these sermons is to realize a little of the intense human warmth and attractiveness which drew so many to this proud and difficult man.

Bernard was one of the great architects of medieval religious culture. He was committed, in a way in which the earlier monastic leaders were not, to the ideal of Christendom, united under a purged but still enormously powerful papacy, militantly engaging with the non-Christian world (he helped to preach the Second Crusade and played an important role in the foundation of the military 'orders' of Templars and Hospitallers); and this commitment is one aspect of Bernard which it is hard to assess. In common with most early medieval theorists, he is content to see the tension between Church and world as satisfactorily expressed in the separation between secular and religious systems of authority *within* Christendom, and in the social and political cohesion of Christendom as a whole over against the heathen (see, e.g., Letter 320). And yet the older view of the monk as a sign and challenge to Christendom itself is not lacking. Part of Bernard's intense inner conflict was grounded in his awareness that the monastic life was as much an absurdity and an anomaly in Christian Europe as anywhere else: the monks were still 'like acrobats and jugglers'; from the world's point of view they were standing on their heads (Letter 90). The existence of Christendom, for which Bernard was so concerned, in whose cause he so spent himself, was ultimately irrelevant to the eschatological pressure of the gospel which he knew to be the real source of his identity and his call. 'I shall play the mountebank', he wrote: 'A good sort of playing which is ridiculous to men, but a very beautiful sight to the angels' (Letter 90; *The Letters of Saint Bernard of Clairvaux*, ed. and tr. B. Scott James, p. 135). This is 'folly for Christ'; very different was the absurdity Bernard so bitterly felt in his political engagement. His conscience was unquiet: he reproaches himself with having abandoned 'real' monastic life for an existence as a 'modern chimaera, neither cleric nor layman' (Letter 326; James, p. 402), a wandering agitator and intriguer. His heart is elsewhere.

To understand the heart of Bernard we must turn to those pastoral writings which most clearly show him as a true monastic *abba.* In them we may find a picture of Christian growth expressive of some of the major insights of monastic tradition, cast in language so rich in poignant imagery that it remains among the greatest achievements of medieval spirituality. Here Bernard is occupied with the analysis of Christian love – so much so that he merits the title *Doctor Caritatis,* the teacher of charity, almost as much as does Augustine. Antony the Great is recorded (*Sayings*, p. 6) as claiming, 'I no longer fear God, but I love Him'; and Bernard brilliantly describes the advance in the Christian life from fearful distance to loving intimacy. Love is not born without a measure of self-regarding fear (Bernard is nothing if not a realist), but it must speedily be left behind. 'Perhaps it can be said that we are called by fear and justified by love' (Letter 109; James, p. 160). In the third sermon (para. 2–3) on the Song of Solomon, he distinguishes between the successive stages of kissing Christ's feet, his hands and his mouth; and the kiss of the feet, with which we begin, is like the kiss of the sinful woman in the Gospel, the kiss of fear and penitence, as we wait prostrate for the Lord's words of forgiveness. And much later on (Serm.LVIII.II), commenting on the text, 'For lo, the winter is past . . . the time for pruning has come' (Song of Sol. 2.11–12; English versions now more accurately read,‘the time of singing’), he writes:

> For us, brothers, it is always a time for pruning, as it is always a job to be done. But one thing I am sure of: the winter is over for us. Do you see what I mean by ‘winter’? it is the fear for which love leaves no room. . . . Summertime is love (*caritas*). As soon as it arrives . . . it is bound to dry up all the wintry showers – all the tears shed in anxiety. . . . Summer too has its showers, but they are sweet and soft ones. What, after all, can be sweeter than tears shed in love? Love weeps indeed, but for loving devotion (*amor*), not for fear; it weeps for longing, it ‘weeps with those who weep’.

The height of summer is love, and it grows from the springtime of Christ’s resurrection, when ‘Jesus, the flower of the field, the lily of the valley’ appears again upon the earth (ibid.8). ‘The summertime has come with Him Who, set free from icy death to live in the spring season of new life, tells us, “Behold, I make all things new”. His flesh was sown in death to flower again in resurrection. The dry wastes, the fields in our valley, soon grow green once more in response to the scent of His freshness’ (*de diligendo Deo* III.8). All human beings are drawn to the love of the creator simply by the consideration of what God has given them *as* human beings – dignity, knowledge and virtue. The grace of God has adorned human existence with the dignity of free will, with self-awareness and with the possibility of seeking and knowing the Creator (ibid. II). But the Christian has a greater and clearer cause for love than this, the drawing of Christ’s sweetness, the gift of new life (ibid. III). All love begins in the debt of gratitude; so love of God begins in a recognition of what God has given to the human race (ibid.V). And the greatest gift, the greatest manifestation of God’s love, is Jesus the incarnate Word.

In some sense, this is ‘self-interested’, of course: it concentrates on what God does for *me*. But Bernard recognizes that love does not exist without a basis of self-love (ibid. VIII). Unless we know what it is to care for and value our selves, we shall never learn what caring and valuing are. Equally, if we stop with caring for and valuing ourselves alone, our love is without *justitia* – proportion, fairness, accuracy; and this *justitia* can come only from loving God. Only in the light of God do we rightly love ourselves and our neighbours (ibid. VIII.25). Bernard's treatise *de diligendo Deo, On loving God,* is organized around a superb analysis of the growth of love, beginning and *ending* in different kinds of self-love, designed to explain how the love of God can permeate and direct all our loves. The scheme (also found in Letter 12; James, pp. 46–7) is fourfold: loving self for self's sake, loving God for self's sake, loving God for God's sake, and loving self for God's sake (*de diligendo* VIII-X). God manifests his goodness by condescending to our self-concern, meeting our selfish needs, so that, from the sterility of self-love for self's sake, we may pass to the love of God for what he does for us. And this also liberates us for loving others more 'justly': our perspectives are broadened, our hearts (in Benedict's phrase at the end of the preface to the *Rule*) 'expand'. Gradually, human love is purified: we begin to love more generously, more as we are loved, the more we 'seek the things that belong to Christ' and strive to penetrate the depths of God's free love. Thus our hearts come to love God for his own sake, for what he is, not only for what he does. But this is not the end: we have to return to deal with ourselves and learn to love ourselves for God's sake. This is to love the self God desires, to love God's will for the self: and so it means the final purging of the will from self-aggrandizement and desire for control. It is 'to be emptied out of oneself, to be brought almost to nothing' (X.27), to accept the reality of God as entirely definitive of one's identity. *Sic affici deificari est:* 'to feel thus is to be divinized' (ibid.). The self is lost in God in that it has no will other than God's.

This is an important definition. Bernard compares the union of self and God with the mixing of water in wine and the heating of iron in fire; he gives no grounds for thinking of an absorption of the finite subject in the infinite. 'Thy will be done' remains the pure prayer of love, a response by one subject to another. 'The [human] substance will still be there, but in another form, another glory, another capacity' (ibid.

18). This is the fulfilling of the commandment to love God with the whole heart and soul, when the needs of the flesh cease to press and body and soul are in perfect harmony (ibid. 19). The needs of the body no longer distract heart and soul from their desire for God: this desire, the longing of the soul, is now, as it should be, uppermost. But this is so far from suggesting that the body is an embarrassing or dispensable appendage that Bernard insists that this harmony is not perfected before soul and body are reunited at the general resurrection. The soul on its own is incomplete and longs for the body; only when the body, risen and glorified, is returned to it can it fully turn in longing to God, turn wholly away from any concern affecting itself (XI. 30–1; and compare *Serm. V in Cant.* 2). Then indeed it can embark on the endless road of proper self-transcendence – 'a searching never satisfied, yet without any restlessness . . . that eternal, inexplicable longing that knows no dissatisfaction and want' (ibid. 33). The soul's journey is without end precisely because it will never be identical with, coterminous with, God.

The relation between God and self is always, in the mature life of grace, face-to-face. 'That glory does not crush me (*non me opprimet*), as I strain towards it with all my powers; rather am I sealed with its imprint (*imprimar*). For when His face has been uncovered, we who behold it are transformed into the same likeness, "from glory to glory", by "the Lord Who is the Spirit" (Cor. 3.18). We are transformed when we are *con*formed. But let no one ever presume that man's conformity to God is a likeness to the glory of his majesty rather than a lowly conforming to His will' (*Serm.* LXII *in Cant.* 5). There is a longer discussion in *Serm.* LXII *in Cant.* (5–10), where Bernard carefully distinguishes between the eternal union of Jesus with the Father, and our union with him. The union of Father and Son is a union of will, the union of the human self with God is a union of *wills* – 'not confused in substance but agreeing in will. This union is for God and man a communion of wills and a *consensus* in love' (9–10). We may compare *Serm.* LXVII (8): ' "My Beloved is mine and I am His". What is beyond doubt here is that this expresses a mutual love between two persons; but in this love we see the supreme happiness of one and the wonderful condescension (*dignatio*) of the other. For this is not the consenting or the embracing of equals.' Thus Bernard resists not only the distorted view which sees the particular human subject vanishing into the Absolute but also the equally wrong idea that a human being can simply confront God as a being on his own level, within his grasp. Just as for Gregory of Nyssa, the life of grace is an entry into a vast new world; but in Bernard it is the face of God in Christ which meets us wherever we turn, in new light, new aspects, not simply the pervasive, pregnant darkness of Gregory's beatitude. Bernard is in his own way defending the significant reality of the created subject and its life and story: the self is a reality which God eternally finds and meets and loves, a face he beholds as it beholds his.

The *de diligendo* concisely and the *Sermones in Cant.* more diffusely treat of the same movement, the purification of love from possessive self-directedness by ever greater openness to the pressure of God's love. Not surprisingly, the theme of Christlike humility recurs time and again in the *Sermones in Cant.* (e.g. XI.7–8, XXV.8–9, XXVIII, *passim,* etc.), and the Letters (e.g. 151; James, p. 220), and is made the subject of a whole treatise, *de gradibus humilitatis, On the Degrees of Humility;* and the *de diligendo* concludes (11, 75) with the picture of Christ coming forth to serve at the heavenly banquet. This is the fullness of humility, the humility of love. Bernard distinguishes what he calls 'humility inspired and kindled by love' from 'the humility generated in us by the truth but having no warmth' (*Serm.*XLII *in Cant.* 6). Accurate self-knowledge very properly makes us humble, but this has nothing to do with the humility of which Christ gives us the definitive example. We need to know ourselves before we can enter the household of God (*Serm.* XXXV–XXXVII, *passim*), but this of itself does not constitute love because it is not free; it is merely the necessary recognition of how things are. For Christ, 'it was by will not by judgement that He was so humble that He presented Himself as something He knew He was not' (*Serm.* XLII.7). Christ's humility is a wholly gratuitous identification of himself with the condemned and suffering, whose lot he had no cause to share. And it is this movement of the will that we are enjoined to imitate (ibid.8). If the awareness of the truth about yourself is humiliating, accept it, *will* it, and act accordingly in loving and selfless service; accept the cost and pain involved. The *compassio* of this humility is the fragrant bunch of myrrh between the breasts of Christ's bride (ibid.11).

Here Bernard turns, naturally, to the consideration of obedience. 'It is little good your being subject to God unless you can also be subject to every human creature for God's sake, the abbot, as the chief authority, or the priors he may appoint. And I would go even further and say, be subject to your equals, be subject even to your juniors (*minoribus*)' (ibid. 9). Even more clearly than in Basil and Benedict, here is the authentic monastic doctrine of obedience, as universal and mutual availability and humble charity. And this is not unconnected with what Bernard writes elsewhere about refraining from passing judgement on others and comparing oneself with others (*Serm.* XXXVII.7, XI.5): the service of others depends on an awareness of the unimportance of the self's status and achievement. And it demands *solitude*, the 'solitude of mind and spirit' that refuses to pry and examine, judge and categorize others, that is always ready to put the best interpretation on the behaviour of others, knowing its frailty so well (XL.5). As Bernard writes in Letter 108 (James, p. 157), he as a sinner has no ground for shrinking from other sinners in disgust. This is Bernard's version of that 'dying to one's neighbour, of which the fathers of the desert speak; but he extends and enriches the notion of 'solitude' *for the sake of love* in his own unique way, to a degree very rare in earlier monastic literature. Although he shared Basil's dislike of hermits (see, e.g., Letter 118; James, pp. 179–90), he possessed a profound understanding of precisely why solitude is the heart of the monastic life and its Christlikeness, and equally of why it is a beginning, not an end, in the Christian life.

Like Augustine, Bernard insists with painful intensity on the need to conquer illusion, to see the self as it is in its poverty, confusion and conditionedness, and then to *embrace* that reality and act accordingly, in a fashion reflecting the self's dependence and insufficiency, its place in a far wider network. More or less unawares, he unites the Augustinian preoccupation with fallenness and powerlessness with the

Greek monastic stress on free will and purification precisely in this model of the two kinds of humility, truth issuing in love, compassion and service understood as growing from the recognition that the self is not a centre of control. The understanding of our condition, of the weakness of the will, does not paralyse but liberates the will's proper exercise in love. Bernard makes more than Augustine of the element of choice, of the constant, deliberate will to sustain love, service and obedience; and this is understandable in the light of the tradition out of which he speaks. Monasticism's emphasis was always on the prosaic process of daily conversion, the decision for God made – joyfully or wearily – time and again in the smallest matters of daily business with other human beings. Augustine's genius is in the wholeness, the sweeping comprehensiveness, of his picture of the believer shattered and compelled by God's violent beauty; the genius of classical monasticism is its recognition of the reality of effort, tedium, painstaking regularities in the believer's attempt to be faithful to his vision, to be accessible to the violent, reshaping love of God. Perhaps Bernard's genius is, briefly, occasionally, precariously, to see and hold these together as he breaks and shares the bread of his contemplation for his brothers, inviting them daily to look for the elusive sweetness of the bridegroom in their life together in the cloister. 'Thy statutes have been my *songs*: in the house of pilgrimage' (Ps.119.54; quoted by Bernard in *Serm.* I. *in Cant.* 9).

6. Ecstasy and Understanding

The Dionysian Heritage

If understanding and love belong together, it is always too simple to oppose a 'mysticism of knowledge' to a 'mysticism of love' in the Christian tradition. We have already seen how hard it is to say even of Clement, Origen or Evagrius that they are wholehearted intellectualists; the same pressure exerts itself on all of them, the pressure of God revealing himself not in 'saving truths' but in saving relation, by means of a movement of sacrificial love. So, when systematic attempts are made to talk about how God makes himself known, it is natural that his 'knowable' and his 'lovable' aspects and activities are in no way divorced. Gregory of Nyssa and others, as we have noted, saw the knowledge of God as essentially a sharing in his loving *activity* through identification in the Church with Christ. And the whole concern of the Greek Fathers and their heirs in the Byzantine Church to avoid any idea of a possible knowledge of God's 'essence', *ousia,* is connected with this conviction that God is never known independently of his loving will to give himself to human beings: there can be no neutral, 'uninvolved' talk of God, no definitions from a distance. This was (and is) what Eastern theology means by a knowledge of God's 'essence' and explains much of its fierce hostility to medieval Western language about the vision of God's *essentia.* Although the Westerners meant something very different from the crudely intellectualist notion attibuted to them, it is easy to see how provocatively its terminology sounds in a Byzantine ear.

Yet both Eastern and Western ways of talking about the knowledge of God were influenced by the same small group of writings, the so-called *Corpus Areopagiticum* – the writings ascribed to Dionysius the Areopagite, Paul's Athenian convert (Acts 17.34). Their alleged authorship (not seriously challenged until the sixteenth century) gave them a near-apostolic authority; and although the distinguished Russian Orthodox scholar, Fr John Meyendorff, has several times persuasively argued that their *real* influence in the East was relatively limited, there can be no doubt that they long enjoyed enormous prestige. In fact, they are likely to be a product of the very late fifth or early sixth century: the first quotation from them appears in 533 and they seem to be dependent not only on the Cappadocian Fathers, but also on the writings of the Athenian Neo-Platonic philosopher, Proclus (who died in 486). They are written in Greek, though it is a very unusual and often barbaric Greek, full of odd turns of phrase and newly-coined words. It is generally agreed that Syria is their place of origin; and their anonymous author seems to have been sympathetic to the party which broke away from the Byzantine Church in dissatisfaction with the 'Definition of Faith' agreed by the Council of Chalcedon in 451. This party is normally, though a little tendentiously, called 'monophysite', since it rejected the Chalcedonian idea that the two natures (*physeis*) of Godhead and humanity were present without mixture or fusion in Christ. The monophysites held that the unity of Christ demanded a unified 'nature' which was both divine and human, and the pseudo-Dionysius' language about Christ certainly suggests this view. It is pleasantly ironical that so vastly influential a writer should have been, by the standards of those he most influenced, a heretic and a schismatic.

The whole of the *Corpus* deals with one question: how does God share his life with creation? Two treatises, the *Celestial Hierarchies* and the *Ecclesiastical Hierarchies,* explain the structure of participation whereby heavenly and earthly realities transmit the divine life down through a descending scale, a hierarchy, at the summit of which stand the supreme angelic orders of seraphim, cherubim and 'thrones'. On earth, 'our hierarchy' of bishops, priests and deacons reflects the heavenly order and, in the liturgy, presents to the 'initiates' (monks, laity and catechumens; Dionysius shares the Neo-Platonic passion for triads everywhere) a symbol of the 'intelligible realities' above (*Eccl.hier.* III.3, V.7, etc.). As Fr Meyendorff comments, this reduces the whole sacramental life of the Church to a system for individual enlightenment (*Christ in Eastern Christian Thought,* pp., 104–6, *Byzantine Theology,* pp. 201–3); it was to have a disastrous effect upon both Eastern and Western liturgical thought and practice. In spite of correctives in both quarters, the notion of sacrament as spectacle or icon came to be widespread and popular and has not a little to do with the universal medieval decline in communicating attendance at the Eucharist. The overall structure of Dionysius' system derives from the elaborate Neo-Platonic systems developed in the fifth century at Athens, and the general principle of an ascent to the 'intelligible' world through symbolic material things and sacred rites is familiar from the *demi-monde* of Hellenistic religious practice. On the basis of the *Hierarchies*, Dionysius' Christianity seems rather peripheral.

However, there is an importantly Christian element in the *Corpus.* Fleetingly in the *Ecclesiastical Hierarchy* (I.4) and more extensively in the *Divine Names (de divinis nominibus),* Dionysius stresses that the structure of participation is not simply a 'natural' fact, but is grounded in the voluntary goodness of God. The Neo-Platonic 'One' proceeds into multiplicity and participation as a matter of course; but the Dionysian God *desires* to share himself. Thus the whole elaborate and fanciful ordering of the world of the *Corpus* does, ultimately, depend upon love, and this gives it its Christian content. God is God, surpassing alike 'language, intuition and being' (*de div. nom.* I.1), 'supersubstantial', not within the order of existing (because existence or 'being' suggests limited and definable life). God is too real to 'exist' as things exist, and his reality is utterly and eternally beyond our grasp; and yet he 'comes out' of himself in *proodoi,* emanations, multiple activities. In these, God manifests himself to and is shared in by creatures: they are the *analogiai,* 'analogies', which lead the soul to God, and it is because of them that God can be spoken of or named at all. The transcendent ground of all is both nameless and possessed of every name (ibid. I.7); no predicate applies to it simply and unequivocally, but every predicate belongs to it. Is there, then, any predicate more true than any other? Yes, since all predicates apply to God in virtue of one fundamental act of 'goodness'. This is the name which sums up all emanations (ibid. III.1). God shares himself in creation because, just as we 'yearn' for him, so he eternally 'yearns' to give himself and to be loved. Dionysius strikingly picks up Ignatius' phrase, 'My *eros* is crucified', and maintains that this divine *eros*, this longing, is fundamental to all we say of God (ibid. IV.12). God comes out from his selfhood in a kind of 'ecstasy' (*ekstasis*, literally, a 'standing outside') when he creates; and his ecstasy is designed to call forth the ecstasy of human beings, responding to him in selfless love, belonging to him and not to themselves. Thus in the created order there is a perpetual circle of divine and human love, *eros* and ecstasy (ibid. 13–14).

This is a remarkable and powerful passage, not least in its application to God of terms which both Neo-Platonist and orthodox Christian would have found highly problematic if not actively offensive. It sets at the foundation of Christian discourse, and Christian experience, the divine *passion* to love and be loved. Fr Sebastian Moore has written recently: 'I sense these days an inadequacy of the notion of "the Will of God" . . . I want another word, suggesting the wanting-to-be of God in our lives' ('Some Principles for an Adequate Theism', in *The Downside Review*, July 1977, p. 206). This seems very close to what Dionysius is speaking of. The insistence upon God's will to love is a feature which serves to 'de-Platonize' the Dionysian picture very radically. Yet it remains true that Dionysius nowhere connects this directly with any christological ideas, and that the revelation of God's 'goodness' is seen as somehow a function of the whole created order in a rather indiscriminate way. And Dionysius' remarks about the Trinity are also puzzling: one passage (*de div. nom.* II.4 ff) certainly implies that the persons of the Trinity are 'emanations' from the primal unity. Although they are the first of all the *proodoi*, they belong on the level of the 'names' of

God, the multiple forms in which he reveals himself. Similarly, at the end of the treatise (ibid.XIII.3), in the course of a long series of statements about what God is not, Dionysius denies that God is either 'one' or 'threefold' (*trias*) 'as we understand it'. It is hard to avoid the conclusion that Dionysius does indeed consider the Trinity to be part of the divine dispensation rather than the intrinsic divine reality. And this means, among other things, that any idea of the intimacy of sonship as the climax of union with God is more or less impossible. The treatise on *Mystical Theology*, which follows the *Divine Names*, is an attempt to give some dim picture of union with God, but it is so permeated with the language of absolute negation that it is not easy to extract from it any strictly theological views. The human *ekstasis* involves the abandonment not only of all sense-experience but also of all 'religious' experience and understanding, in order to enter the divine darkness (*de myst. theol.* I; cf. *de div. nom.* IV.11). This is impressive, and immensely important (recalling Gregory of Nyssa and anticipating very significantly St John of the Cross); but it lacks (as Gregory and John do not) any attempt at offering a theological rationale of the *state* (not simply the 'experience') of union with God.

It was left to a succession of commentators in East and West to give a reading of Dionysius which smoothed away some of these more ambivalent features and developed more clearly and more theologically his central insight. Foremost among the Eastern commentators was Maximus of Scythopolis, 'the Confessor' (so called for his sufferings in the Orthodox cause), who died in 645. Probably the greatest *systematic* thinker of Eastern Christianity, he produced a theology both Christocentric and metaphysically serious which has had a very important influence on Eastern Orthodox dogmatics up to the present day (and especially in the last thirty years). Maximus develops at length the idea of *perichoresis*, 'mutual communication' or 'reciprocal motion', between divinity and humanity in Jesus (*Disputatio cum Pyrrho*, PG 91, 337C, 344–8; *Ambiguorum liber*, ibid.1040, 1049–52, 1060A, etc.), so as to suggest that the reciprocal movement is one of *kenosis*, self-emptying. The eternal Word first empties himself of his divinity to become man, then empties himself of instinctive human passions in accepting suffering and death. Human beings are called to share in his human *kenosis,* responding to the divine *kenosis:* we must empty away our lives in order to grasp what he has done (*Capita theologiae et economiae* I.55,PG 90, 1104 BC). 'By the *kenosis* of the passions, a man may make the divine life his own, in the same degree in which the Word of God willingly accomplished in Himself, by the dispensation of grace, a *kenosis* relative to His own pure glory when He became truly human' (*Orationis dominicae expositio,* PG 90, 988). God's *kenosis* of love, his *ekstasis* from his own nature in becoming human must be answered by human love and human *ekstasis* into the divine life (*Quaestiones ad Thalassium,* 64, PG 90, 724B – 728D, *Or.dom.expos.,* ibid. 877A–880A); in a characteristic expression of Maximus, the human destiny is to become by grace what God is by nature (e.g. *Amb.liber,* 1308B). And this is achieved by the indwelling of the Spirit, who realizes in us the sonship of Christ (ibid. 1345–8).

Maximus, then, gives to Dionysius' speculations a clear foundation in Christology (just as the Dionysian 'hierarchies' are given by Maximus a meaning more clearly related to a Christian doctrine of creation by the eternal Word). Alain Riou, in a brilliant study of Maximus (*Le monde et l'église selon Maxime le Confesseur),* has argued that Maximus effects a kind of synthesis between the more dynamic and personal approach of Origen or, still more, Gregory of Nyssa, and the static, iconic picture of the Dionysian writings (pp. 38–9). Maximus' scheme preserves a balance between the natural and the personal: Origenist dynamism alone can turn into a romantic glorification of instability, and Dionysian hierarchicalism can simply exclude initiative, divine and human, from the order of things. Maximus' subtle understanding of the relation of Christ's person to his two 'natures' opens up the possibility of a genuine reconciliation. And although Riou's division is rather too neat, it points to one of the most important features of Maximus' work, its character as a 'metaphysic of grace' – a serious essay on the structure of reality that yet succeeds in having at its heart the free loving activity of God in Christ, the self-yielding of God on the cross.

Aquinas (*c.* 1225–1274)

If it seems strange that Thomas Aquinas should find place in a chapter dealing with the theologians of 'ecstasy' – Aquinas who was in so many ways so relentlessly prosaic – that is a reflection of a fairly widespread misunderstanding, both of Aquinas and of the notion of 'ecstasy'. Essential to many areas of Aquinas' thought is the possibility of what we might call *perichoresis,* the kind of relation in which each term has a kind of life or existence in the other. It has been rightly said that the notion of love, *caritas,* is the great unifying theme of the *Summa Theologiae;* and it is so because it is a theme which makes possible that bridging of the gulf between the Creator and finite reality which is Aquinas' purpose. 'Since love causes the object of love to exist in the lover, and *vice versa,* it is right that the effect of love should be seen as a mutual indwelling (*inhaesio*)' (S.T.I.2ae.28,ii.concl.). Love involves 'ecstasy', in that the lover is taken out of himself or herself; and the most authentic 'ecstasy' is the wholehearted willing of the good of the loved one, not the movement of possessive love which goes out to the other only to bring back something for the self (ibid. 28.iii,resp.dic.). And the 'ecstatic' character of love is confirmed by 'what Dionysius says: that "the divine love produces ecstasy" and that "God Himself is said to experience ecstasy on account of love." So, since any kind of love is a sort of shared likeness of the divine love, so it is argued, it seems that any kind of love will produce ecstasy' (ibid. 18.iii.contra.). Perhaps, then, it is not so misleading to see Aquinas as a theorist of ecstasy; although the word is very rare in his writings, the notion of 'presence in the other' is central. We shall see how this affects his account of knowledge in general, and of religious (experiential) knowledge in particular.

Aquinas' use of *intellectus* and *intellectualis* is one of the things which suggest to the modern reader an aridly cerebral system. When we read that human beings are in God's image in virtue of their 'intellectual' nature (S.T.I.93) or that contemplation is primarily an 'intellectual' activity (ibid. II.2ae.180.i.concl.), it is natural to conclude that what is being proposed is some kind of impenitently Hellenic system.

However, *intellectus* for Aquinas is a rich and comprehensive term which is totally misrepresented if understood as referring to the discursive intellect. Its central meaning seems to be that it designates the human subject as receptive and responsive: receptive to the impressions of 'intelligible form', discernible order and structure, in the realities it encounters, and responsive in its *engagement* with objects, working on them and willing things about them. *Intellectus,* then, means 'understanding' in a very comprehensive sense; and it involves a genuine union of knower and known correlative to the union of lover and beloved. The life of the *intellectus* involves a transition of the object into the subject and is fulfilled and complemented by the life of the will (which is characterized at its summit by (love) in which there is a kind of transition of subject into object, since the subject 'tends to' the object as it is in *itself* (S.T.I.16.i.resp.dic., 83.iii.resp.dic., II.2ae. 66.vi.ad I,etc.). The *intellectus* longs for truth exactly as the will longs for good; and in the important discussion of God's will in S.T.I.19, it is made very clear that will and understanding are inseparable.

> Will is consequent upon understanding. Natural things exist by acting through their particular form, and similarly understanding is the understander acting through an understandable form. Now any thing has an aptitude for this natural form; and when it does not possess it, it tends towards it, and when it does possess it, it rests in it. . . . Thus it is that an understanding nature has a similar aptitude for its good (i.e.what is proper and beneficial for it) as grasped in understandable form, so that if it has it, it rests in it, and if it does not have it, it seeks it. And both these are activities pertaining to willing. So that there is willing in any entity that has understanding (ibid. I.19.i.resp.dic.).

Precisely because understanding involves a relation and a *movement* of the subject towards something – involves what modern Thomists usually call 'intentionality' – it belongs with will; and will has to do essentially with desire, approbation, valuation, all elements comprised in the idea of love.

God is his own object, his understanding is internal to his existence and he needs no external datum to give form to his understanding: he is never passive, because his being and his doing are one. He is 'pure act', and his movement of understanding and love is therefore primarily towards himself. But finite subjects have a gap between being and doing, and so need to be stimulated, moved, need to be receptive: their motion will always be directed to a reality beyond themselves. God understands and loves because he 'rests' in his own perfect freedom and sufficiency; we understand and love because constrained by our need to be filled, by the outward drawing of external reality.

God rests; but he rests in his 'goodness' which, for Aquinas as for Dionysius, is itself an overflowing and ceaseless movement. It is this *bonitas* which makes incarnation proper for God: the nature of created humanity into the divine life, is the highest form of self-communication possible for God (S.T.III.I.i.resp.dic.). It is often remarked that Aquinas manages to discuss subjects such as grace, contemplation and knowledge of God without any reference to Christ; and this is seen as a central failure in his system considered as a *Christian* metaphysics. But there are several points which might qualify such a judgement. First of all, Aquinas simply does not believe that grace is given only to those actually conscious of the work of Christ: for him it can properly be discussed without explict reference to the incarnation, simply as a case of God's gracious activity in relating to his creatures. The incarnation reveals the ground and rationale of this – Christ's 'headship' of all (ibid. 3.8.iii). It is, as the discussion makes clear, the way in which, as a matter of fact, God imparts himself in grace and goodness, but the fact of that imparting, its character and consequences, does not require direct consideration of this. Aquinas' detailed discussions of grace as 'deifying' and as involving the gifts of the Holy Spirit and the indwelling of the life of the whole Trinity should warn us against supposing that he is any way 'naturalizing' or trivializing the doctrine. It is worth noting that his discussion of grace in the earlier *Summa contra Gentiles* (III.150) makes use of the text from Ephesians 1.4–6, which speaks of the 'predestination' of believers in Christ, and that

S.T.III.24.iii and iv pick up the same text and the same theme. Grace flows to us because of God's eternal election of Christ as redeemer.

Grace as God's overflowing *bonitas* is thus the foundation for all knowing of God. We know beings only in so far as they are 'in act', *existent* in the sense of impinging upon us, being real in the world and so acting and relating. God is supremely and purely existent (he is, as Aquinas repeatedly insists, *esse* itself, the pure act of existing), and therefore purely active; and he 'impinges upon us' in all our reality, whether we know it or not. But this self-gift in grace is a gift to human beings in their awareness and responsiveness – in their 'intellectual nature'. So the knowledge of God which arises from contemplative prayer is 'intellectual', and contemplation is 'intellectual' in character. However, it cannot be thought of as *exclusively* a matter of understanding; indeed, the implication of the discussion is that there is no such thing as an exclusive 'matter of understanding'. Understanding culminates in the union of knower and object, and this is an occasion of 'delight'; and it begins because of a willed search, a 'feeling around' for an adequate object, an *appetitio,* a desire to be completed by an *other.* So all understanding begins and ends in *affectus,* feeling, and contemplation is a specially clear instance of this, beginning in the conversion of the will towards God and ending in the sheer and unqualified fulfilment of the vision of God in glory after this life (ST.II.2ae.180 i,v,vii,viii). Aquinas here stands very near some of the great monastic writers of the previous generation. Bernard's close friend, William of St Thierry, for instance, makes use of the distinction between the 'love of desire' with which contemplation begins and the 'love of delight' in which it ends, in his beautiful treatise *On Contemplating God (de contemplando Deo).* And this is a valuable reminder of a long-obscured truth, that Aquinas is the heir of the classical monastic tradition, and that it is a grave mistake to read him exclusively from the perspective of later medieval scholasticism. His method may be radically different from that of earlier monastic theologians: yet he is often nearer in his concerns to Bernard, say, than to the relentlessly abstract schoolmen of the fifteenth century.

Aquinas is very cautious about complex analyses of the contemplative experience. In S.T.I.180, he puts the question 'whether different kinds of activity properly belong to contemplation' (art.iii), and replies in the negative. He several times refers back to the discussions of contemplation by Richard of St Victor, one of the foremost speculative writers of the twelfth century, who was much given to detailed subdivisions of the activity of prayer, and gently suggests each time that, valuable as Richard's distinctions may be, they belong strictly to the activities which put one 'in the way' of contemplation and can in any case be more simply rendered (art.vi.ad.3). What Richard is inclined to speak of as different *kinds* of contemplation, Aquinas describes as the stages leading to proper contemplation, which is a unified and simple thing. The mind moves from observation of sense objects to the inchoate activity of understanding, and thus to an *understanding,* an 'intellectual' grasp, of sense objects; then to the understanding of *intelligibilia,* transcendent or universal truths, as they are contained in sense objects, and so to these universal non-material structures as 'reason' grasps them. But only after that does contemplation begin: the understanding has started with sense experience and advanced to rational comprehension, but contemplation transcends sense and reason alike. It is the *intellectus* simply being receptive to the ultimate reality of universal and transcendent truths, which is the divine truth itself (art.iv.ad 3). This constitutes a perfectly clear repudiation of 'intellectualism': contemplation is seen as the understanding purified to a point of pure receptivity. What Aquinas is describing is a process of gradual enlargement of the understanding's scope; it becomes less and less determined by any created reality, material or immaterial, and so more and more exposed to the direct determination of the divine act of grace and self-communication. It is the condition in which nothing is *happening* in the mind but what God is doing.

So when Aquinas speaks of the mind's involvement in sense experience as an obstacle to serious contemplation, he is not working on a simple body-soul disjunction but admitting that, since the mind and soul are entirely bound to the body and its senses, there cannot be on earth a condition in which *only* the activity of God is working in the subject. He might have said much the same about the activity of the reason 'processing' sense experience as an obstacle. This is a recognition that contemplation, although in important respects continuous with the rest of the life of the understanding, is essentially *odd.* It is 'an activity appropriate in the highest degree for human beings' (I.2ae.3.v.resp.dic.), yet it is strange and singular, and unlike other human acts in being determined by grace alone. It is this which underlies the deeply sound advice of, for example, the *Spiritual Letters of Abbot Chapman,* and other classics of direction, concerning the problems arising out of the sheer emptiness and even absurdity of many people's experience of contemplative prayer. 'In the intellect there is *no perception at all,* if the prayer is pure. One might call it an act of ignorance, or a sensation of idiocy!' Thus Chapman (op.cit.,p. 59), who is followed by Sebastian Moore (art.cit.p. 201): 'The shift from *the concept* of the infinite to the experienced and verbally suggested *touch* of the infinite is the most devastating mind-shift conceivable. Its expression is the near-nonsense of Chapman, a very special, gracious and pastoral kind of near-nonsense.' This is exactly Aquinas' point about the difference between the last two stages in the growth or ascent of the understanding, the passage from 'rational' consideration of intelligible realities and the direct contact with divine truth; at the final level, there is no concept for the reason to work on, therefore no work for the reason to do. 'In "contemplation", the intellect is facing a blank, and the will follows it' (Chapman, op. cit., p. 76). Hence the experiences of (sometimes terrifying) disorientation which regularly accompany the contemplative enterprise.

Aquinas touches briefly on this in 180.vii.ad. 4; how can contemplation be a 'delight' when it involves struggle and hurt, as when Jacob wrestled with the angel? He refers to St Gregory the Great's exegesis which sees the wound as a weakening of worldly love: Jacob will limp henceforth, resting his weight on his good foot, the love of God, and avoiding as far as possible treading on the weak foot of worldly love. Contemplation is a struggle (ibid. ad 2) because the 'contrariety' of external things upsets the soul's simple activity, and this is inevitable so long as the contemplative is in his corruptible body. As at *present* constituted, the life of the senses is an impediment, and contemplation is a battle. But the body's destiny is glory, the heavenly condition in which the simplicity of the soul will simplify and purify the body's life. No longer will the senses distract, because the 'light of glory' in which the soul sees and knows will transfigure the whole 'world' of the subject – the heavenly body and its perceptions, whatever they may be (S.T.I.2ae.3.iii,4.vi; III.3.45.ii; Suppl. 82–85). Aquinas is careful in 180.vii to speak only of the body's *present* ('corruptible') state.

Here, then, is the first thorough philosophical exposition of the experience of confrontation with God in contemplative prayer. Origen and Bernard (and many others) had written of the soul's advance to *direct* intimacy with God, the kiss of the mouth; Gregory of Nyssa and Dionysius, of the breakdown of conceptual structures and images as God is approached. Augustine describes the mind's capture by the drawing of God's beauty. Aquinas, so much the 'dullest', the least impassioned, of all, draws these themes and much else together in his metaphysics. No less than Augustine, he sees the enterprise of prayer as beginning in awakened longing; with Gregory and Dionysius, he detaches the knowing of God from any kind of conceptual acquaintance and so, like Origen and Bernard, is concerned to reflect on what it is to experience God without 'mediating' realities in the way. His conclusion explains the fact, recognized and described by all the previous writers, that this experience can be difficult, painful and bewildering; here the 'understanding' has no work to do except to keep itself still and receptive. It faces an emptiness of ideas and pictures which may or may not be filled at different times with some sense of an object or interlocutor; Aquinas says little about this. In heaven ('in our native land', as Aquinas always puts it), there will be the entirely satisfactory 'sense of an object', there will be *light;* but meanwhile, the only guarantee that it is *God* who is present to the self is that nothing else in particular is so present, and that no consistent set of words or ideas (about God or anything else) is at work. It is a darkness in which the only significant human act is the will's movement of desire – the bare readiness to abide in hope and longing in the darkness, to be content with nothing else because anything else would be *less* than God.

In the technical language of scholastic philosophy, this is 'knowledge by connaturality' – knowledge based on God's presence in the self. God (so to speak) finds himself and knows himself in the human subject, because he has entered its life. This is what is meant by speaking of contemplation as a 'supernatural' condition – an expression both puzzling and disturbing to some. It is 'supernatural' because only intelligible in the light of God's initial self-gift to the redeemed in general and to the still and receptive understanding in particular; and because the understanding here functions in a way that is not 'normal' for it. This can very easily be taken as meaning that contemplation is 'abnormal'; and it may be asked how contemplation can be thought of as 'appropriate in the highest degree for human beings' if it is abnormal. But the truth is that, while Aquinas is passionately concerned about the integrity and wholeness of 'natural' life and never wants to create gaps into which 'religion' can be inserted, he still sees the *last* 'end of man', the ultimate goal, as a self-transcending action – the natural life in its entirety gathered up and taken beyond itself in the act of desire for God and exposure to God. As he often said, grace does not destroy nature but brings it to perfection. In this case, it is a matter of the natural *intellectus* having the function of responding to what is there, confronting it; so that it reaches its highest point when it responds to what is most totally, unequivocally, consistently *there:* God. Yet the sheer thereness of God *is* so total that the understanding can only receive, it reaches its destiny by coming to stillness and silence. It becomes clearer and clearer that its 'nature' is to be 'immediately aware that we are concerned with what is not a matter of our choice but what is thrust upon us' (D. M. MacKinnon, *The Problem of Metaphysics,* p. 163; the whole of chapter 13 of this work is pertinent to this discussion). There are, as Jacques Maritain argues in his magnificent work on the Thomist theory of knowledge (*The Degrees of Knowledge,* pp., 280–3), analogies with moral and artistic 'knowing' here; but contemplation remains a supreme and so a unique case. In all the confusion and uncertainty of the contemplative experience, so long as the will holds the understanding turned to God, the Creator can pour his life into the finite self and so find his image there. And as Augustine delighted to repeat, it is the image of being, knowing and loving joined in one simple act, in the self as in God.

Meister Eckhart (*c.* 1260–1327)

At least one of Aquinas' disciples was to take the theme of the passivity of the understanding and press it to the extreme point at which nervous authorities began to speak of heresy. Johannes Eckhart was, like Aquinas, a Dominican, who held positions of some seniority in the Order (he was for a time Provincial of Saxony) and gained a wide reputation as a preacher, not only as a speculative thinker and teacher. Most of his work survives in sermons, a very large number of them in German, and there are also extant collections of 'counsels', apophthegms and brief anecdotes. He was evidently a popular and influential, though a distinctly controversial, figure. A Papal Bull of 1329 condemned several opinions which had been attibuted to him, and he had in his lifetime faced charges of heresy: he was accused of confusing the created and the uncreated, of teaching dangerous doctrines of divine immanence and implying the uncreatedness of the soul. He defended himself fairly successfully against these charges and appealed to Rome against the condemnation of his compatriots; but he was dead before the final negative judgement came from the Holy See. There can be no doubt that Eckhart's dense and involved language and his love for paradoxical and startling phrases and images make it unusually difficult to construct a clear picture of his thinking and to decide what exactly, among the opinions with which he was charged, he would have asserted and what he would have denied. However, recent work has made it clearer that Eckhart stands very firmly in the Thomist tradition, for all his revisions and idiosyncratic emendations of it; he is not simply a 'mystic' (as many have thought) propounding a vaguely oriental pantheism at odds with the mainstream of the Christian tradition.

He follows Aquinas in employing the Aristotelean distinction between *intellectus* as active and as passive – the 'active intellect' laying hold of phenomena and presenting them to the 'passive', in which their 'form' is assimilated. Eckhart describes this in a characteristic image as the active intellect pouring images into the womb of the passive intellect until the latter becomes pregnant, 'conceives' the object as intelligible (*German Sermons,* III). Thus in prayer what happens is that the active intellect is superseded and the agency of God himself is the inseminating force; and since God is 'simple', what is offered to the mind is not a profusion of images and concepts but a single all-embracing reality. The intellect's response is, then, a simple, completely focused act: the mind is refined to a point of concentration. In this condition it becomes what it ought to be, the *scintilla,* 'sparkle', in which God's own light is reflected back to God.

It was Eckhart's language about the *scintilla animae* that caused most puzzlement and suspicion to his contemporaries. He speaks of the soul in this state as 'a power untouched by time and flesh' (*German Sermons* VIII), as like God in its perfect unity and simplicity, as the image of God's solitude. It is, as Eckhart so often repeats, virginal. Yet it must also become wife and mother, for God has destined the soul to bear his Son. When the soul is virginally pure of all deeds, recollection and images, she is fit to conceive by the Holy Spirit and bring forth the eternal Word (ibid. IV, VIII, XXVI, LXII, LXXIX, etc.): 'The moment the spirit is ready, God comes in without any hesitation or delay' (ibid.IV). God cannot refuse the petition of the virgin soul. Not surprisingly, imagery of this sort provoked questions: it could and can be read as a kind of revived gnosticism, treating the soul as naturally divine, waiting only for its summons to return home. There is certainly some provocative language about the eternal being of creatures in God in, for example, the fifty-sixth of the *German Sermons,* and the subtle distinctions which Eckhart attempts to draw between participation and identity cannot have been much clearer when the sermon was preached than they are now. Nevertheless, it is clear that he sees the soul as a secondary and derivative reality. Like all the creatures, it has a heart of pure being which simply reflects God and so 'is' God; there is no substantial difference between what is true of the reflection and what is true of the original – except the fact that the original *is* the original and has behind it a depth and density of reality lacking in the reflection *as* reflection.

This is not gnosticism or pantheism, but a serious statement of the idea that the soul is *capable* of simple receptivity to God and that in grace it does indeed take on the shape of that which it contemplates. It is not, therefore, a position radically different from that of Aquinas. Eckhart is found of emphasizing that the intellect thirsts for *being* as its object; it is made to be moulded by the sheer thereness of things, and so it will only be satisfied with the well-spring of all being, the eternal thereness of God. Yet God never shows himself completely in his purity to finite persons in this life. The mind 'finds no rest at all, but goes on expecting and preparing for something still to come but so far hidden. . . . Only the truth will do, and this God keeps on withdrawing from it, step by step, with the purpose of stirring up its enthusiasm' (*German Sermons* III). Eckhart, then, sees Christian growth as a constantly deepening attention to the pure, simple singleness of God, an increasing readiness to 'let go' of self-directed thoughts and pictures. It means, as he says, letting the soul become a 'desert', an emptiness in which there is space for God to work. All external devotions are merely adjuncts to this; in an Ascension Day sermon (*German Sermons* LXXXVI.1) on the text 'It is expedient for you that I go away', he boldly describes the seven sacraments and the 'human shape of our Lord Jesus Christ' as obstacles to spiritual growth, the sort of remark which won so much odium from some of his contemporaries and so much admiration from woolly Romantics in the nineteenth century. But in the context of the sermon, it is clear that he is not in the least questioning the saving efficacy of sacrament or incarnation, but rather objecting to facile, limited and materialistic ideas of grace. Some souls are trapped in a sacramental theology entirely preoccupied with outward forms and regulations and need to be reminded that the sacraments are there to point beyond themselves. As for devotion to Christ's humanity, Eckhart associates this with a piety which is unhealthily interested in visions, messages and assurances of God's special providence; and this is to limit and confine God. The true following of Christ is the following of the *whole* Christ, the eternal Word as well as the historical figure. 'It is expedient for you that I go away': salvation and sanctification are not worked by the recollection of a historical character, but by entry into the whole life of the Son, into 'the union of the holy Trinity'.

Yet what Eckhart has to say about the Trinity is often very obscure. Like Dionysius, he sometimes suggests that the Trinity is a kind of second-level divine existence. The Trinity is God (*got*) but not Godhead (*gotheit*); the persons are God in 'conditioned nature' (*German Sermons* VIII). As Trinity, God works, acts and relates, but as 'Godhead' he is at rest, at one, indescribable and immutable (ibid. LVI.). And the union of the soul with God is ultimately with the simple *gotheit:* God has to put aside quality, personality and modes of being for him to be able to 'look into' the soul, to enter the 'castle' of the soul and dwell there. 'He cannot do this as Father, Son and Holy Spirit as such, only as – yes, as something, but not this or that' (ibid.VIII). Yet, as in eternity the *gotheit* blossoms into Trinity, so, it seems, in the soul does it flower into the birth of the eternal Word, Eckhart's favourite image. The Word 'is in the Father as the intellectual image of His divine essence and the reflection of His divine nature . . . it is with the Father as the person of a son. It is in the soul as the likeness of the equal persons and modes of God' (ibid.IX.). Eckhart could be read as saying something like this: that to attain union with God, all modes and models have to be set aside, even the *doctrine* of the Trinity; but having arrived at that nakedness where the naked reality of God can enter, the soul is fertilized into divine life, a reflection of the trinitarian life. In other words, Eckhart is not arguing that the divine 'life' is separable from the divine substance in the sense that it is merely an accidental efflorescence of it. God eternally acts and lives (as Trinity) and is also eternally at rest, eternally uttering his Word and eternally silent.

Thus he does not offer any kind of 'absorption mysticism' in a straightforward sense. Absorption in the simple essence of God is not the goal but the beginning of the life of grace, it is that out of which the abounding and fruitful energy of trinitarian relations springs, in the soul as in eternity. Eckhart's often startling erotic imagery has its place here. Father and Son 'wrestle' to beget the Spirit (ibid. XVIII); the Father embraces his own 'nature' in the darkness, 'playing' with and in the Son, so that their play takes shape as the Holy Spirit (ibid.LVIII). The soul gives birth to the person of the Word 'when God laughs at her and she laughs back'; the Son and the Father thus delight in each other, 'and this laughter breeds liking, and liking breeds joy, joy begets love, love begets the person [of the Word], Who begets the Holy Spirit. This is how He [the Word] wrestles with His Father, (ibid. XVIII). Those who imagine Eckhart to have taught nothing but unqualified passivity in the spiritual life have ignored the force and significance of this remarkable sexual language. God is at once still and fecund, and the soul meeting God unites with both his stillness and his fecundity, with his trinitarian movement of begetting and relating; it is 'made one with the naked Godhead of which the blessed Trinity is the self-revelation' (ibid.LXXVI.i) and so is still, but also can know and do all things by God's working in it (ibid.).

The soul comes to this union by laying aside *all* its selfish desires and all its expectations: 'Seek nothing at all: neither understanding, nor knowledge, piety, "interior life", peace – seek only God's will' (ibid. IV). Eckhart insists that union with God is not primarily a special kind of religious experience. The end of the life of grace is to find God in every experience and activity, to be 'everywhere at home'. The *Spiritual Instructions* declare that 'you should not greatly value what you feel, but what you love and desire' (20), and that 'if a man were in rapture like Saint Paul, and knew a sick man who needed some soup from him, I should think it far better if you abandoned rapture for love' (10). 'Heaven is at all points equidistant from earth' (*German Sermons* LXIX): God is not 'more' to be found in specifically religious occupations. The balance of contemplation and action is indispensable (*Sayings* 33), and the Godlike life is accessible here and now for the person who genuinely lives by self-forgetfulness (ibid. 21). Poverty of spirit, the subject of several of Eckhart's sermons and tractates, means a complete renunciation of reliance on consoling and meaningful experiences in prayer. All that matters is the faithfulness of love, will, desire, intention to the naked reality of God, the faithfulness which takes us to the heart of God's silence and at the same time frees his life to work in us. 'Grace comes only with the Holy Spirit, it carries the Holy Spirit on its back. It is nothing static, but is always developing, flowing straight from God's heart. . . . It makes the soul share God's own form' (ibid. 6).

Eckhart is at least as much poet as metaphysician – perhaps all the better a metaphysician for being a poet. In depth and imagination, he stands alone among his theological and philosophical contemporaries; the condemnation of his thinking came from far smaller souls than his own. But his importance for our present study is chiefly in his insistence that union with God is a reality affecting the whole of experience, not merely its religious moments. The foundation upon which all else rests is the displacement of the self's longing for dominion and satisfaction; when this occurs, in *or* out of prayer or religious practice, the self enters into God's life and 'works God's works'. What matters is not 'ecstasy' in the common sense of abnormal spiritual experience but the ecstasy of understanding, the transition of subject into object, the setting aside of self in order to let the observed and understood reality act without impediment. The self when made naked and poor is free to go forward to God and be welcomed into God. Eckhart is in fact filling out much of Aquinas' scheme, working through the implications of the 'object-less' activity of the understanding which Aquinas speaks of. If the understanding is to leave behind all forms and pictures, all that is less than God, it must abandon the notion that God is bound to particular kinds of experience. If the will is rightly directed, if the self is receptive, he is to be met everywhere. This certainly does *not* mean, for Eckhart, that the enterprise of contemplative prayer is superfluous, since it is in the 'inactivity' of such prayer that we most clearly and fully grasp what it is to meet God-in-act. Contemplation is the source from which flow 'living works', the transformation of motivation; it is what makes possible the grace of encountering God everywhere. The contemplative life, for Eckhart, is by no means an uninterrupted absorption in prayer; like God's own life, it is both rest and overflowing abundance in activity, a life in which prayer provides the central purifying and directing reality that will save outward works from sterility.

Dead creatures, says Eckhart, differ from living ones because they can only be moved from outside; living means moving according to will, being moved from within. 'Those human activities which have their origin within, where God moves by His own power . . . are divine works and useful works' (*Sayings* 32). Eckhart repeatedly draws attention away from external achievement to concentrate upon the springs of action and has hard words for those who perform 'works' – devotional or charitable – without a foundation in true contemplative poverty of spirit and self-forgetting. He is not 'internalizing' the Christian calling or disparaging activity as such, but demanding the recognition that activity is inseparable from motive and desire. He is simply following through the long tradition which we have been considering, the tradition which insists that the conversion of desire lies at the centre of Christian life and that without it more activity is at best sterile and at worst destructive. His insistence that the source of Christian activity must be *God* is a sharp statement of a concept which would have been familiar and acceptable to Antony, Augustine or Bernard, or Aquinas; his divergence from Aquinas is perhaps chiefly in the lack of attention given to the reality of created agency. It is easy enough to understand the accusations of pantheism and 'absorption mysticism', easy enough to see why Eckhart has been acclaimed by some as a stray Hindu in the Christian fold, breaking out of the dogmatic constraints of Catholic orthodoxy. But, when we have readily granted the unclarity and ambivalence of so many of Eckhart's expressions, it remains true – as this chapter is designed to suggest – that he stands well within an authentic Christian tradition. Christian life is, for him, conversion of behaviour grounded in the transforming of desire, the naked receptivity of the self to God's graceful act, the conformation of the self to the eternal Son, and so a growth into the life of the Trinity. And this cannot be simply reduced to a purely Neo-Platonic or essentially Vedantic pattern.

Eckhart's real problem was the lack of a vocabulary. Western Catholicism by 1300 was rapidly losing the means to express theologically the basic principle of its life, the *ekstasis*, emptying, displacement of self in response to the self-emptying love of God, the communion of God and humanity by the presence of each in the other. It was losing the sense of Christian experience as growth in direct encounter with God, growth, therefore, in obscurity, pain and struggle; there was less realization that the roots of theology lie in such experience and that Christian speculation is properly inseparable from engagement of a personal and demanding kind with the paradoxes of cross and resurrection. As the Middle Ages draw to a close, the chasm widens between intellect and will, between the scholastic professionals of theology and the poor servants of God. The contemplative was offered next to nothing for the theological elucidation of his life. And so it was that the theological revolution when it came (almost two hundred years after Eckhart's death) was a violent counter-attack, a desperate attempt to reclaim the territory of theology for the realm of experience and engagement. It was a search, seldom successful but constantly serious, for the lost art of understanding. And for all the hostility of the Reform to even the greatest of the scholastics, the ironic truth is that Aquinas and Eckhart had sought that same art.

7. The Sign of the Son of Man

The End of Christendom

The late Middle Ages witnessed a marked degeneration of Christian thought and practice alike over large areas of the Christian world. The intellectual life of the schools was characterized by an increasing rationalism – not, in this case, an intellectualist optimism of the Eunomian kind, but the exact contrary, a deep pessimism about the capacity of the reasoning subject to abstract beyond the immediate data of experience. The prevailing view-point was 'nominalism', which affirmed that 'generic' names and concepts, talk about the nature or substance of things, were purely a matter of convention. There could be no certain (that is, experiential) knowledge of realities outside the realm of sense experience. Knowledge was seen as 'acquaintance', pragmatic contact. *Religious* knowledge, therefore, was, from a purely natural point of view, impossible. This could issue in two different conclusions. Either we suppose that faith has nothing to do with the knowing of the rational subject and is exclusively a matter of will (responding to some incalculable divine agency); or else we hold that true and certainly knowable propositions are miraculously delivered to the Church and promulgated as authoritative dogma. Of course, the latter can, at one level, be seen as a variant of the former, requiring simply a willed commitment to obedience to the Church's authority. The close connection of faith with the will is a central theme in the thought of the great fourteenth-century

Franciscan, Duns Scotus, for whom knowledge of God is essentially the willed human response to God's willed self-disclosure: will rather than understanding (*intellectus*) determines faith. But it was another Franciscan, William of Ockham, who, rather later in the century, was to develop the idea of religious knowledge as primarily assent to authoritatively revealed propositions. Not surprisingly, many of his followers were to be found in the fifteenth century among the most ardent defenders of absolute papal authority.

Both conclusions had grave effects in the sphere of spirituality. The exaltation of will over *intellectus* naturally went hand in hand with a certain subjectivism and individualism in the life of the spirit. What was of basic concern was the response, not indeed of emotion, but of private consent to God – a simple movement of will, leading to the relationship in which God and man alike 'will well' to each other. It is by no means a view remote from that of Aquinas; but the significant element which has fallen out of the picture here is Aquinas' conviction of a certain continuity between the knowledge of things and the knowledge of God. The Scotist position moves the knowledge of God decisively out of the area of general discussions of what it is to know; and although Aquinas and those who in greater or lesser degree followed him accept that the understanding operates eccentrically in knowing God, they do not deny that there is still a family resemblance between this and its other operations. The effect of such a denial is ultimately to put faith beyond discussion and so to emphasize the subjectivity of the religious discovery of truth. As for the Occamist emphasis upon the centrality of revealed propositions, this has the effect of severing any possible connection between what theology may say and the experiences of believers. Theology becomes a static analytical discipline, concerned with the rational relations between ideas: it is perfectly possible to be a theologian without being engaged in any particular discipline of Christian living. And Christian life becomes something lived in isolation from the world of intellectual questioning; it is, again, privatized, placed beyond discussion.

All over Europe, the fourteenth and fifteenth centuries produced a remarkable flowering of 'mysticism', a great concern with the experience of pilgrimage towards God. Eckhart's fellow-Dominicans, Suso and Tauler, developed his views on spiritual poverty and the 'spark of the soul'. In England, Richard Rolle of Hampole in Yorkshire wrote about the tangible consolations of the spiritual life, while the anonymous writer of *The Cloud of Unknowing*, that brilliant little summary of 'Dionysian' ideas, warned against reliance on such things and emphasized the primacy of receptive blankness in prayer. Walter Hilton's *Scale of Perfection* set out a detailed analysis of the stages of growth in the life of prayer; and the female recluse, Julian of Norwich, unforgettably recorded her *Revelations of Divine Love*, visions of a unique immediacy and profundity concerning the nature of God's utterly sacrificial concern for his creatures. In the Low Countries, Ruysbroeck transmitted a scheme of Eckhartian type to a wider audience; numerous new fraternities and communities both lay and clerical grew up; and the Augustinian Thomas à Kempis composed his *Imitation of Christ* in a reformed religious community of this sort, the house of canons at Agnietenberg. Yet none of these saw himself as a 'theologian'. Many are explicitly hostile to intellectual speculation, the word-spinning of the schools; many are familiar with the technical vocabulary of scholastic thought and will on occasion employ it. Yet they are consciously and deliberately tangential to that tradition in a way in which Eckhart, say, for all his idiosyncrasy, is not. Eckhart is still wrestling with scholastic terminology in order to say something for which the scholasticism of the day gave little space; the later writers more or less abandon the struggle. The chasm has become too wide.

It is, of course, possible to see this late medieval interest in the will as a legitimate development of one aspect of the Augustinian tradition (though Augustinian Platonism comes in for severe criticism from Scotus and his followers). We have seen how Augustine, especially at the end of his life, reduces the springs of Christian living almost exclusively to the blind pulling of desire. What he never does, however, is to deny the destiny of the whole of the *mens* to communion with God: will or love (as the *de Trinitate* suggests) is that which directs memory and understanding from self to God.

The other 'faculties' are *practically* subordinated to will, but they are not separated from it or even seen as swallowed up in it. Will alone – by definition – is not knowledge, and so its operation is never the working of the whole human subject. It may be forced into the central place in Christian experience by the frustration of memory and *intellectus*, but it remains part only of the whole joint enterprise of 'intentionality', direction-towards-the-other, in the subject. Thus, to understand the practical primacy of the will as an ultimate superiority is not genuinely Augustinian. To the Scotist conviction that knowledge yields to love, the Thomist will obstinately reply that there can be no love independent of understanding (however incomplete).

These debates may seem remote to an age which no longer thinks in terms of a clear threefold division in subjectivity. Yet we are familiar enough with ethical and psychological trends which accord central importance to the motion of the will as the most significant and valuable element in human subjectivity. The existentialist exaltation of will is only an extreme instance of a widespread unwillingness to allow that the will is necessarily *constrained* in the public and social world and so bound to conscious adaptation, self-modification, reflective and deliberate activity. If human possibilities are not limitless, the will must reason if it is not to be constantly frustrated. But if this is so, the 'absolutism' of the will is bound to be restricted to a wholly private sphere, where alone it is free from constraint: it can operate at liberty in a world of private beliefs (though even these will in fact be constructions related to and constrained by public reality). Christianity, committed (as I have argued) to the public, the social and the historical, cannot ever be reduced to a purely voluntaristic religion. Public fact, however ambivalent, makes a difference to it; and that 'difference' is the degree to which the normal processes of knowledge and reflection are bound up in it. As an 'historical' religion, it is not bound to claim that history can offer its coercive demonstration, but it *is* bound to recognize that history is a necessary part of its construction, and that the truth or falsity of certain historical propositions is material to it. So, to retranslate this into more scholastic language, what the understanding receives from the public and material world is ineradicably associated with the object of faith. The equivalence of faith, knowledge and will serves to render belief invulnerable, at the cost of making it finally incommunicable. And these are not questions of merely archaeological interest, as even a slight acquaintance with twentieth-century theology will show. The lure of invulnerability still attracts.

The Young Luther

Much of the perennial interest of Martin Luther lies in his understanding of the relation between 'worldly' fact and transcendent saving truth. It was for some time fashionable to emphasize his debt to the nominalist philosophy of Ockham and others; but it becomes more and more clear that the Reformers generally are struggling to find a defence of the relation between theology and experience against the critique of the schools. Luther was not in any sense a philosopher, and, whatever the prevailing influences were in the philosophical world of his day, his response to them was not that of a professional. He was not a humanist, a cultivator of classical learning determined to reinstate Plato, as some reforming Catholics of his generation were. He was far more identified with those whose interests lay in the rediscovery of Scripture and primitive tradition; he read Paul and Augustine for himself. He was also, as a young friar and teacher, sympathetic to the tradition of German mystical writing of the previous century and a half, especially the writings of Tauler and the anonymous *Theologia Germanica* (which he translated into German). Such contemporary influence on him as there was came from these non-scholastic circles. Nominalism may explain some features of some of his thinking, but it cannot be seen as a mainspring. Luther's real location is among the literate 'primitivist' Catholic reformers of the day, those who wished to see a wholesale cleansing of the Church and its schools which would restore to theology its proper character as a discipline of *interpretation*, engaging with Scripture and the early Fathers, not simply of *analysis*, the organization of the conceptual structures of late scholastic speculation.

The order of Augustinian friars or 'hermits' to which Luther belonged was generally sympathetic to this trend. Erfurt, where Luther was professed, was a strict and orderly house, and the new and active theological faculty at Wittenberg where he became a professor was staffed by members of the order. The first dean of the faculty was the then vicar-general of the German Augustinians, Johann von Staupitz, a man of profound theological and scriptural learning and a pastor of great sensitivity. Luther, who did not bestow praise lightly, retained a lifelong veneration for this remarkable man, whose sympathy had exercised a real restraining influence upon him. Staupitz's resignation of the vicariate in 1520 (he died as a Benedictine in 1524) was unquestionably a landmark in Luther's deteriorating relations with the order and the Church in general. To all appearances, then, Luther in his young manhood in the second decade of the sixteenth century was surrounded by relatively congenial brethren and colleagues – a radical, but in a modestly radical atmosphere. It seems very odd that the problems caused by Tetzel's crude propaganda for the sale of indulgences in 1519 should have turned Luther into a major revolutionary. And of course it is a caricature (though still a popular enough one) to see Luther's revolt in this light. The crisis of 1519 *was* a crisis because it compelled Luther to draw together, to weld into a single weapon, the thoughts of many years and the torment of many years; it drew from him the strong statement of what *he* had found to be the good news of Christian preaching and a challenge to the Church to affirm it or refuse it. The Church prevaricated; Luther read this prevarication as refusal and reacted accordingly.

The Reformation cannot be understood at all without some sense of the agony of Luther's interior battles in these years leading up to 1519. It is given to mercifully few people in the Christian Church to experience directly and intensely the meaning of words and phrases that are, for most believers, clichés. Luther looked, with rare simplicity, into the face of the God he was told to serve and *hated* what he saw. God was a righteous God – that was taken for granted – and he demanded conformity to his righteousness and condemned failure to conform. He demanded whole-heartedness; but how could the endlessly self-regarding, self-observing, self-dividing human soul *produce* such simplicity? Nothing in human action and motivation could be clear; by what right can a person ever satisfy himself or herself that an action is 'good'? By no right; Luther found this out through years of self-torture in the confessional. Scripture enjoined 'penitence' – *poenitentiam agere,* 'do penance', was the Vulgate translation of the evangelical 'repent'. And if sin was a nightmare of daily failure and doubt, so penance was a nightmare of struggling to find the possibility of unequivocally good acts by way of recompense – which would themselves be open to the same agonies of doubt about motivation. How was it possible to be pleasing to God? As Luther often put it in later years, this experience was an experience of hell, of a condition of moral and spiritual hopelessness. The God who presides over this appalling world is a God who asks the impossible and punishes savagely if it is not realized – punishes here as well as hereafter (on these experiences, see *Martin Luther,* an anthology of short texts edited by G. Rupp and B. Drewery, pp. 4ff). The righteousness of God, *justitia Dei,* is a threat hanging over the whole of every human life. The expression itself for a time produced a pathological revulsion in Luther (Rupp and Drewery, p. 6), and there was 'scarcely a word in the whole of Scripture which had a bitterer taste than "penitence" ' (from a letter to Staupitz in 1518; in *Reformation Writings of Martin Luther* (vol. 1, ed. B. L. Woolf, p. 57). The most significant fact about Luther is that, in these years, he *hated* God.

Staupitz provided one important source of relief. He was able, as a Greek scholar, to assure Luther that the New Testament's conception of penitence was a far richer thing than the pinched and formalist medieval *poenitentia:* it was *metanoia,* conversion, the redirecting of the whole personality, not an act to be performed to satisfy the heavenly despot. This new conception, which Luther himself confirmed by his studies in the Greek text, was a stimulus to his fertile intellect. Encouraged by the sympathy of his superior, he continued his biblical studies, struggling to extract from the texts of

Scripture the vision of a gracious God; and at some point between 1513 and 1516, the final clue fell into place. At this period, Luther was lecturing on the Psalter and the Epistle to the Romans and, especially in the latter, was more and more brought up against the problem of God's 'righteousness'. Precisely when the breakthrough occurred is hotly debated (Gordon Rupp's definitive study, *The Righteousness of God,* contains a full discussion on pp. 129 ff) but is hardly of the first importance. What is clear is that during this period Luther realized that the righteousness of God was not 'active' – that by which God condemns – but 'passive' – that by which he finds us acceptable by making us righteous. God's *justitia* is what God gives us in order to make us his: it is grace and not condemnation. Luther writes movingly to Staupitz about the 'paschal' quality of this experience, the overwhelming sense of a deliverance from bondage (Woolf, op. cit., p. 58). This was his *metanoia,* the conversion which made new the whole world, which revealed a new God: a God who could be loved, prayed to and trusted even as he smote and killed. A strange and a terrifying God, yet a source of life and hope.

In 1518, Luther was called upon to defend several of his propositions in public disputation at Heidelberg; and the theses which he presented on this occasion (extracts are to be found in Rupp and Drewery, pp. 27–9) provide an invaluable summary of this new theology, the 'theology of the cross', as Luther termed it, in contradistinction to the 'theology of glory' which he saw as characteristic of late scholasticism. The *theologia gloriae* 'calls evil good and good evil' (thesis 21): it looks on outward forms only, and so fails to perceive the strange and contradictory reality of God's working. The *theologia crucis* is accurate vision, which is prepared to confront without flinching the terror of God's judgement, to look at the 'evil' of doubt, dereliction and fear and call it good. 'Without the theology of the cross man misuses the best in the worst manner' (thesis 24): the annihilating effect of 'law', reminding human beings of their impotence, must never be softened by a legalism which treats law as a simple task to be performed. And likewise, human wisdom and rationality are properly used to recognize our poverty for what it is and must not be perverted into an instrument of human power, a speculative device for uncovering divine truth. 'Law', the experience of the categorical and unsatisfiable demand in the relation of humanity to God, is appointed as judge and executioner: what it cannot kill is Christ. So what it strips away and destroys is all in us that is not Christ (thesis 23). Theology deludes itself if it finds the *invisibilia Dei,* the hidden things of God, clearly manifest in the world or in experience. The pivotal statement of the Heidelberg Disputation is the great twentieth thesis: 'He deserves to be called a theologian . . . who comprehends the visible and manifest things of God seen though suffering and the cross.' The 'proof' of this thesis refers to 1 Corinthians 1 – the weakness and the folly of God – to establish that God displays himself 'visibly', publicly and historically, only as the humiliated and tortured Jesus, because men and women have perversely believed that their rationality can carry them speculatively into the invisible realm of divine truth. God overthrows speculative theology by making himself a *worldly* reality.

Here Luther is, in one respect, the child of his empirically minded philosophical precursors. Knowledge is a historically conditioned affair, it is not intuitive grasp of transcendental states of affairs. But to take this seriously means equally to reject the idea of privileged authoritative propositions delivered from religious illumination. It means to grasp that any speech about God is speech about an *absence:* the world we inhabit does not present God to us as simple fact. God is made known to us in the cross, in a man's death in abandonment. So for all human beings God is to be met in what 'contradicts' or opposes him, in sin, in hell, in pain and guilt and lonely despair; theology begins here, in the Godless world at its most extreme. *Only* here, in what negates and mocks all human conceptions of God, can God be himself. Paradoxically, the real and absolute transcendence of God can only be understood in circumstances and experiences where there are no signs of transcendence, no religious clues. It is, as Luther again insists in the 'proof' of thesis 20, useless to consider the transcendence of God, 'His glory and majesty', independently of the human encounter with him in the godlessness of the cross. Here, where all theological speculation, all conceptual neatness and controlledness fall away, God is simply God. It is an experiential and historically oriented restatement of the tradition of negative theology: God himself is the great 'negative theologian', who shatters all our images by addressing us in the cross of Jesus. If we are looking for signs of God's authentic life, activity and presence, we shall find them only in their contradictories, in our own death and hell, as in Christ's. The *theologia crucis* concerns itself only with the visible, the worldly; but it grasps and values the worldly for what it truly is, the garment of God. The *theologia gloriae* seeks to escape from the worldly and so turns its back on God. 'Philip [in John 14.8] spoke according to the theology of glory: "Show us the Father". Christ forthwith set aside his flighty thought about seeing God elsewhere and led him to himself, saying: "Philip, he who has seen me has seen the Father" ' (proof of thesis 20; Rupp and Drewery, p. 28).

Some Lutheran scholars of an earlier generation, conscious of the links between the Luther of these years and certain aspects of the mystical tradition, tended to regard the *theologia crucis* as no more than a stage in Luther's progressive emancipation from 'Catholicism'. However, the classic work of Walther von Löwenich, *Luthers Theologia Crucis,* first published in 1929, definitely established the theme as fundamental to the whole of Luther's thinking. And, as Gordon Rupp remarks in a foreword to the English translation of the fifth (1967) edition, von Löwenich's revisions show a more generous appreciation of the real continuities between Luther and the whole tradition of German contemplative discipline. That Christian authenticity begins from the wreckage of all human efforts to contain or control God is a view which we have seen to be central to the mainstream of Catholic tradition. What Luther (and the classical Protestant world in general up to the present century) objects to is the perversion of the contemplative approach into a 'mysticism' which imprisons God again in a set of human experiences. Eckhart's insistence that no particular, special religious experience mediates God unambiguously, that there must be no seeking after 'inwardness or peace' for its own sake, is very close to Luther's thinking. And if Luther can be read in the light of Eckhart (and of Eckhart's disciples, Suso and Tauler, whom

Luther studied extensively), it is clear that the reformer cannot simply be interpreted as an enemy to contemplative theology and practice: he is, rather, an uncomprising champion of the innate iconoclasm of contemplation.

Does this mean, then, as some critics have held, that Luther reduces Christian life to an exercise of interpretative vision sustained by pure will? That he is at heart a nominalist, incapable of taking seriously the idea of real, experiential participation by human beings in the life of God? Such a criticism misunderstands very seriously the genuineness of Luther's concern with development and change in the Christian life, attributing to him a view of 'righteousness' as entirely external, entirely in the mind of God, which he would have repudiated sharply. He does indeed see sanctity as 'passive', worked in and not by us, but that does not render it an empty word. God works, and his work is experienced by us; the point is that the experiencing of it has to be interpreted strictly and exclusively with reference to the paradigm of God's work, which is the cross. Faith begins in the experience of *accusatio sui,* alienation from self, guilt, the sense of condemnation: an experience which becomes *metanoia* when it is seen as a taking of the cross, standing where Christ once stood, under Law, under wrath (Rupp, *The Righteousness of God,* pp., 167–73). This is the essence of Christian humility, the recognition of one's total poverty, the 'emptying out' of human wisdom and human righteousness. It is a true 'coming to onself', in that (characteristically of the *theologia crucis)* it calls things by their proper names, penetrates the appearance, the illusion of being successful and at home in the world,and unveils the truth of human exigency. It is an experience, without any doubt; but not, in the conventional sense, a 'religious' experience. It is human experience 'retold' in the light of the story of the cross, experience confronted by the proclamation of God's wrath and so changed from mere self-flagellation into repentance. Nor is it a momentary or a transitory experience, solved and removed by justification. The duality of Christian experience – wrath and grace found together in the cross – persists throughout life (see Rupp and Drewery, p. 27, and Regin Prenter, 'Holiness in the Lutheran Tradition', in *Man's Concern with Holiness,* ed. M. Chavchavadze, pp., 127–8), and there is no grace without the prior stripping away of illusory self-complacency. Every moment of grace and forgiveness rests upon the experience of *accusatio sui;* before you can be reconciled, you must see your alienation. This is the meaning of that well-worn and much misunderstood saying of Luther's that every believer is *simul justus et peccator,* 'righteous and a sinner at one and the same time'. It is clearly articulated in chapter 24 of Luther's major treatise on *The Bondage of the Will.* Here is the underlying structure which makes experience *Christian* experience, the daily felt polarity between rejection and acceptance, distance and intimacy, guilt and grace, united with the sense of God's double working in the event of the cross, the double manifestation of wrath and mercy. To know forgiveness in the midst of hell because of the cross of Christ is the criterion of true Christian faith. 'Having entered into darkness and blackness I see nothing; I live by faith, hope, and love alone and I am weak, that is, I suffer, for when I am weak, then I am strong' (from the Weimar edn. of Luther's works, the *Operationes in Psalmos,* vol. V, 176.16 ff; quoted in von Löwenich, op.cit., p. 83).

Sanctity, the 'passive' sanctity with which Luther is concerned, is inseparable from the experience of *Anfechtung* (dereliction, *tentatio* in its strongest sense), since God 'can manifest his power only in weakness' (Table Talk, Dec. 1531, recorded by John Schlaginhaufen, in *Luther's Letters of Spiritual Counsel,* ed. and tr. T. G.Tappert). It is the constant disposition to 'resignation', acceptance of the hell of self-doubt, that opens the way to grace. And the suffering that results from sin because the real sinner, the unconverted man, thinks himself happy without God; whereas it is the sense of God's absence that is the pitch of the believer's agony (see Rupp, op. cit., pp., 189–90). Quite pragmatically, the believer is upheld and supported by the knowledge that Christ himself passed through this hell and thereby consecrated it to God, as he consecrated all human experience (an echo of familiar patristic views); as he sanctifies the waters of baptism by his immersion in the Jordan, so he sanctifies the floods of suffering (*in Psalmos;* Weimar edn. V, 619,14; also ch. VII of a celebrated early work, the *Fourteen Comforts for the Weary and*

Heavy-Laden, in Woolf, op.cit., vol. II, pp. 41–2, where exactly the same image is used). In Christ we see holiness fully present in the most extreme *Anfechtung:* the fact of Christ's perfect oneness with the Father is not touched by his *experienced* agony. Christ's cross is, from one point of view, the supreme demonstration that holiness is nothing to do with mere states of mind.

Faith and Experience

Faith, then, is living in *Anfechtung* with trust and hope, a 'conviction of things not seen' in a very strong sense. It is the confidence that reality is not the same as what is being felt at any given moment (see von Löwenich, op.cit., p. 82). Where a human being stands in relation to God cannot in any way be deduced from his or her subjective state, any more than it can from speculative thinking. Even when, in later years, Luther wished to say more about the positive content of faith, he still took for granted the essential importance of the gulf between faith and experience. It may be, as the older Luther implies (for instance, in the *Lectures on Genesis*), that beyond the darkness and paradox of *Anfechtung* there is a subsequent assurance, a more tangible sense of reconciliation and security. But von Löwenich (op.cit., p. 88) cautions against too literalist a reading of this later material, reminding us of the pastoral concern always present in Luther's theology; and, in any case, Luther would have denied that there was any point at which the believing soul becomes invulnerable to *Anfechtung*. There is no neat biographical sequence of a *period* of darkness followed by a *period* of illumination. The illumination is the process by which the darkness itself comes to be seen as intelligible, as the source of life and grace, by daily striving to live in, abide in the darkness. The 'proof' is not internal testimony, but the whole life of the believer.

Luther can say with conviction that it is by experience that the Spirit teaches us (see, e.g., the preface to his commentary on the *Magnificat;* Woolf, op.cit., vol.II, p. 191). But here it is clear that 'experience' is being opposed not to faith but to reason on the one hand and specialized 'mystical' experience on the other. The experience which teaches is the day-to-day life of trust, the life which is its own evidence; nowhere is Luther's distance from late scholasticism clearer than here. Experience is very definitely reinstated as a theologically significant matter, yet without any surrender to a belief in privileged private intuitions. And, as von Löwenich demonstrates (op. cit., pp., 95 ff), it is *trust* which is the bridge between faith and experience. Trust is and is not a 'willed' thing: it can never simply be reduced to a groundless movement of will, yet it is not the issue of compelling rational demonstration. It is a disposition which both feeds and is fed by 'experience'. In the Christian context, trust would not exist without the conviction, based upon the understanding of Christ's cross, that reconciliation with God is truly offered and bestowed in Christ, the conviction of God's action *pro me,* God on my side, on my behalf; and that historically centred conviction preserves Christian experience from anarchic subjectivism. As the reform grew and advanced, Luther had severe difficulties in dealing with the left wing of the movement, the prophets and charismatics, whose visions and inspirations provided justification for extreme and violent methods of purifying the Church's life. His response to them is precisely in terms of the givenness of the cross as the touchstone of Christian understanding; he was genuinely shocked by the claim to direct 'conversational' contact with God and evidently saw this as a near-blasphemous trivializing of the terrible majesty of the Creator, the unendurable glory which has to be veiled in the flesh of Jesus crucified. In a letter to Melanchthon (13 January, 1522; in Rupp and Drewery, op.cit., pp., 75 ff), Luther instructs his friend to ask the 'prophets' 'whether they have experienced spiritual distress and the divine birth, death and hell'; if they can produce no more than a catalogue of spiritual sensations, they are not to be heard. 'The sign of the Son of Man is then missing.' *Crux probat omnia,* all things are to be measured by the cross alone (Weimar edn., v, 179.131). It is both the triumph of 'experiential' theology and the wreck of a mere theology *of* experience.

Because Christian identity is not to be specified in terms of particular passing states of experiences, Christian life for Luther is pre-eminently a life of freedom. God's freedom from both rationalist and 'mystical' projections secures human liberty: if God is free to act and to be present in all the diverse conditions of human life, men and women are free to go and find him there. This is the impetus behind Luther's violent assault on the monastic life. For him, the existence of separated communities, performing distinctive activities, wearing distinctive garments, made a nonsense of the Gospel, since it implied that God's concern was with the extraordinary. It is a striking witness to the limitations of the monastic theology in which Luther's generation had been educated that this shallow caricature emptied the religious houses of half a continent. It is easy enough to show what a perversely mistaken valuation of monasticism is involved in the reformer's attack: but the moral and theological passion of the attack points to a deep malaise in the religious life of the time, sharply felt within as well as outside the cloister. Luther himself continued to wear the habit until 1524; but in 1525, he signified that he had broken absolutely with his former life by following the example of many other former religious in those years and marrying (an ex-nun, Katharina von Bora). His personal and theological affirmation of the Christian possibilities of life outside the cloister, in family and society, was for him an unavoidable consequence of the whole style of theological interpretation he had evolved. For countless others it was a message of liberation – perhaps cheaply and glibly apprehended by some, but not the less genuine and effective. Those who see Luther as the first exponent of a 'secularizing' theology forget the profound and costly understanding of faith which underlies his 'conversion to the world'.

As early as 1520, his treatise on *The Liberty of a Christian Man* set out in depth and detail what was the nature of Christian liberty. Its foundation is the assurance that particularized obligations have nothing to do with faith, that any conception of Christian life which reduces it to 'technique, is to be rejected (chs.4 and 5; Woolf, op. cit., I, p. 358). The Christian is the 'lord of all', both king and priest, in virtue of the promises of God in the Gospel (chs.14 and 15; ibid., pp. 364–5) and of the bridal union between Christ and the soul which faith effects (ch. 12; ibid., p. 363). God shares in the humiliation and sinfulness of humanity when he receives the faithful soul to himself, and humanity is endowed with the freedom of Christ (ibid.). No work, then, is to be done for the sake of earning salvation; but this does not mean the overthrow of discipline or of Christian service. Faith must grow. A person may be entirely and finally justified in his or her soul, but there is more to the person than the soul. Since we are material beings in a material world, holiness must be worked out in the body, in public and social life, assimilating the historical, developing life of the body to the already existing state of the soul (ch.20; ibid., pp. 369–70). And, at this stage, Luther is still perfectly willing to allow the propriety of many traditional ascetical practices (ch.28; pp. 377–8). The Christian must make the whole of his life Christlike, internally and externally. So, although he is free internally, he must be ready to be 'bound' for Christ's sake, to take on gratuitous observances of discipline so as not to despise others (ibid.; it is perhaps worth mentioning that Baron von Hügel in the early years of this century recommended the regular use of the rosary to Catholic intellectuals – or would-be intellectuals – for precisely the same reason). More significantly, just as God leaves his own state of transcendent freedom to be 'bound' in the service of humanity in the person of Jesus Christ, so the believer too must undergo an 'incarnation', a 'becoming human'. Christ had no need of worldly good deeds to make him holy; so, like him, the believer 'ought voluntarily to make himself a servant and help his neighbour. He should associate and deal with him as God has done with himself through Christ' (ch. 27; p. 376). We must in every sense *be* Christ to our neighbour, in a 'free, eager, and glad life of serving . . . without reward' (ibid.). Human beings are called, in fact, to a double act of 'self-transcending'; rising to God by faith, stooping down to the needs of others in self-forgetful love. The essence of Christian freedom is that the believer 'lives not in himself, but in Christ and his neighbour' (ch.30; p. 379).

The way in which Luther here draws the distinction between outward and inward may be rather naive, but the substantive point concerns the indivisibility of the Christian act of self-transcendence. Both with respect to God and with respect to men, the believer undergoes a 'displacement' of the self and its self-oriented desires. As for Eckhart or indeed, Gregory of Nyssa, it is one and the same reality which underlies the internal turning to God and the external serving of the world. There is *one* conversion; the Lutheran 'conversion to the world' has little to do with the fashionable notion that God is to be found in the world or in the service of others *rather than* in prayer or interiority. If conversion does not begin in each person's private hell, in the meeting with God the crucifier and the crucified in the depths of the heart, there is no ground for the second level of conversion. But once the self has been dethroned in the interior victory of God's righteousness, there is only one possible 'translation' of this into bodily life, and that is the service of the neighbour. The self that is killed by God in order to be made alive must experience this death in the social, the public world at the hands of other human beings. The daily dying, daily taking of the cross, is precisely this exposure of the self to the devouring need of others. It is 'active holiness'. The cross is borne internally in *Anfechtung,* externally in enduring whatever may be attendant on the state of life in which we find ourselves. Luther's anger at the monastic rhetoric of 'bearing the cross' by means of the religious vows grows out of his conviction that the cross is never *chosen.* Both internally and externally it is encountered as a thing imposed; otherwise it becomes a human invention, a technique, a work (see von Löwenich, op.cit., p. 84). Religious life negates the cross by institutionalizing it, controlling the range of possible demands that may be made. Paradoxically, what had been seen as the highest, the paradigmatic, vocation, was regarded by Luther as intrinsically incapable of being a vocation at all.

Luther's concept of vocation (finely discussed in Gustaf Wingren's study, *The Christian Calling*) was a radical and significant modification of all previous thinking on the subject. At one level, Luther is denying that vocation ever means the call to a state of life with circumscribed duties derived from religious principle. It is always the call to serve God where you are, in whatever state of life you may be. Any job may be a vocation to the extent that we see it as a possible place for response to God: what makes it so is not any 'religious' quality in the work itself, but the selfless faith and love of the person performing it. Duties and obligations are prescribed by the actual worldly conditions in which work is to be done, the function it must fulfil, not by a theological underpinning (Luther would not have been impressed with a 'theology of work', one suspects). In society, the believer is not distinguished by what he does, *nor even* by the way he does it. The Christian life is so interwoven with the ordinary life of persons in society as to be indistinguishable from the life of others (Wingren, op. cit.; see also his later book, *Gospel and Church*, pp. 143–4). Christian existence, like all other works of God, is hidden, it cannot be described in terms of a catalogue of visible deeds and qualities (von Löwenich, op. cit., pp. 123–5). Any task which can be shown to meet some human need is sanctifiable, by that very fact alone.

The manifold weaknesses of this view have often been set out. Luther, notoriously, leaves almost no place for a criticism of society and its needs and offers no criteria for resolving the question of whether a socially defined task can ever be *in*capable of being a 'place for response to God'. How many can take seriously Luther's defence of the Christian hangman? And how many find the concept of the Christian soldier as unambiguous as he did? Luther's ideal society was a relatively uncomplicated system, in which the social utility of more or less every job would be clear; but this was a long way even from the Germany of the early sixteenth century. Luther was aware of growing complexities in society, but had little fresh to say to them (he had a very strictly medieval loathing of usury, for instance). His social theories have not worn well in the post-medieval era, and his picture of the person in society is, even by medieval standards, remarkably passive and static. That there is a proper (and sanctifiable) creativity in social and political life, that men and women may be called to become (in the modish phrase) 'the subjects of their own history', is a consideration beyond his horizon for most of the time. Yet the implicit denial of theocracy remains of major significance: Luther never envisages the Church as a pseudo-state or as the governing force of a society. What is to be done in human society cannot be determined by the Church, and

Christians are not to confine their activities to religiously prescribed duties. Christianity, in other words, is not a moral code, but the gift to humanity of a wholly transformed life. The idea that such a new life might involve moral and political discrimination represents a step which, in practice, Luther acted upon but for which he was unwilling to give theological grounding. But at least it should be clear that Luther is far from confining the gospel to the private sphere; his views may be passivist but they are not simply individualistic, or what was later to be called 'pietist'. It is in this perspective, incidentally, that Dietrich Bonhoeffer is most adequately understood, as a man who had very deeply assimilated the Lutheran doctrine of vocation and was prepared to take the further step into political discrimination, in a particularly costly way. The relation between 'worldly holiness' and the 'secret discipline' of faith in Bonhoeffer's prison writings is a clear echo of Luther's understanding of the hiddenness of the springs of Christian living; and the living before God as those who can live 'without God' which Bonhoeffer commends is a characteristically Luther-like paradox. Bonhoeffer is one of the great interpreters to this century of the meaning of *Anfechtung.* He found himself in a lonely and trackless place of the spirit, oppressed with conflict and ambiguity, and made of that a place of response to God, in trust and in action. Those tempted to dismiss Lutheran spirituality as passive and privatized would do well to consider how deep were Bonhoeffer's roots in his own tradition.

For all the accusations of preaching a 'forensic', 'verbal' or 'external' idea of righteousness, Luther does believe the grace of God to be a transforming agency, shaping us into his likeness (see, e.g., Rupp, *The Righteousness of God,* p. 181). The treatment in *The Liberty of a Christian Man* of the theme of becoming Christ for others is a plain indication of this, as is the statement in the preface to the newly translated Epistle to the Romans (1522) that faith makes us 'altogether different men in heart and spirit and mind and powers' (Rupp and Drewery, p. 95). How could it not? Faith is the emptying-out of self, and it is that emptying that first makes possible authentic love. Faith by its very existence effects newness of life, and its end is that condition in which faith and love wholly remove the self's obstruction to God's working. *Simul justus et peccator* indeed: Christian joy exists only in virtue of Christian hope, the promise of final reconciliation for the whole person. Yet in the bodily life of man, Christian growth is a reality. As we have noted, Luther's division between the entirely 'saved' soul and the unstable body is crude, and there is in his thought a strand which sees the body's history as fundamentally a striving not to fall away from the enduring righteousness of the soul, rather than as a progress in its own right. But this is merely to allow that Luther, in the unsatisfactory anthropological terms he had inherited, gave strong expression to the Pauline tension in Christian experience between what is given and what must be realized; and since the soul daily lives in the extra tension between trust and 'experience', there is no room for a complacent piety or any sense of spiritual achievement. If Luther has little time for the construction of plans or maps of advance in the life of the spirit, it is not for lack of concern with the elements of conflict in the life of Christian discipleship.

Luther's task was to reconstruct a Christian theology which took seriously the *intractable* quality of God's nature and work, over against the mechanical religiosity and sophisticated agnosticism of the late Middle Ages. He was able to use much of the armoury of Catholic tradition itself in his enterprise – Augustine most obviously, others, like the Rhineland mystics or St Bernard, more obliquely; but to his eye the reconstruction of belief was a matter demanding a comprehensive critique of the tradition and the outright rejection of large areas in it. And because he confronted a Catholicism preoccupied with external and juristic conceptions of authority, it is not surprising that he won only the most negative response from the hierarchy of his Church. The Reformation put a question of the utmost gravity to all Christians, a question about the continuity and dependability of human response to God. It affirmed that the Church was capable of error; that no amount of scholastic tidiness could guarantee fidelity to God; that there was in the Church no secure locus of unquestionable authority. It pointed eloquently to human brokenness, the failure of reason and order. But it did so only to claim triumphantly that the Church's security lay in this very failure, in the insecurity and un-rootedness which drove it always back to its spring in the Word made broken flesh. Against the self-sufficiency of Christendom is set – rightly and decisively – the cross. To Christians looking for a sign, an assurance, it offered only the 'sign of the Son of Man', God hidden in the death of Christ. As the ground of theology (and everything with it) it offered, not a reasonable deduction, but an experience of hell, from the conviction that only in hell could the goodness of the good news be heard for what it was. Luther is a reminder to Catholic and Protestant alike that the strength of Christianity is its refusal to turn away from the central and unpalatable facts of human self-destructiveness; that it is there, in the bitterest places of alienation, that the depth and scope of Christ's victory can be tasted, and the secret joy which transforms all experience from within can come to birth, the hidden but all-pervading liberation.

8. The Secret Stair

The Way of Denial

The restoring to the Christian world of a theology both rooted in and critical of 'experience' was not the exclusive work of the Reformers alone in the sixteenth century. The Catholic and monastic world itself experienced a far-reaching renewal from within – a renewal only marginally related to the institutional reforms of the Council of Trent, but bearing much fruit in the public life of the Church in the century that followed. It is perhaps predictable that this should arise in one of those areas of Europe least touched by the Reformation: Catholic Spain, relatively recently united, full of fresh confidence, victorious at last over Islam, and lately embarked on vast colonial expansion. It is not an agreeable society; very few wealthy and expansionist societies are. Its treatment of the substantial minorities of Moors and Jews in Spain is as appalling as its treatment of the natives of Central and South America. But its aggressive confidence at least provided a security in which the exploration of Catholic spirituality could be pushed to radical limits by the least triumphalist, the most un-confident of the saints of that age, John of the Cross (1542–91). St John is a prophetic figure whose stature is all the more clear and marked against the background of his place and time. He had been into the same desert, the same hell as Martin Luther (though neither would have relished the comparison) and perhaps lived there even longer; he was capable of unmasking – simply by his own integrity and faithfulness – the delusions of the competent and successful in the religious world. He died in disgrace, after a long history of strained and bitter relations with his order. For him, as for Francis of Assisi, the movement he had done so much to nurture was to turn on him in hostility in his last days. In middle life, he suffered at the hands of those in the order who resisted his reform and spent several months as a prisoner in the hands of the unreformed party; in his old age, those who had supported the reform itself stripped him of all his offices and confined him to a remote priory. There is some evidence that accusations against him had been lodged with the Inquisition; certainly many of his later writings have disappeared without trace, and the Inquisition evidently continued to regard his work with suspicion for a considerable time after his death. There exists a defence of some of the saint's controverted propositions, sent to the Inquisition by Fray Basilio Ponce de Leon of Salamanca in 1622 (to be found in vol. III of *The Complete Works of St John of the Cross,* tr. and ed. E. Allison Peers, pp. 382–434). He has never been regarded as a simple or a 'safe' writer in monastic circles right up to the present day; Abbot Cuthbert Butler's classical essay on *Western Mysticism* took great pains to demonstrate that St John was in no way representative of 'mainstream' Western spirituality, and Abbot John Chapman, who was to become one of the greatest twentieth-century interpreters of the saint, wrote that 'for fifteen years or so, I hated St John of the Cross, and called him a Buddhist.' He adds, characteristically: 'Then I found I had wasted fifteen years, so far as prayer was concerned!' (*The Spiritual Letters of Dom John Chapman O.S.B.,* ed., with a memoir, by Dom Roger Hudleston, O.S.B., p. 269). St John has not ceased to be a controversial and provocative figure.

Unlike his contemporary and close associate, St Teresa of Avila (1515–85), St John did not relish the public scene or the exercise of authority, and he most certainly did not set out to be 'controversial' or revolutionary. He and Teresa alike were forced into their radical positions by the sheer pressure of their own understanding of the demands of the vocation; both found that the Carmelite order to which they belonged failed to embody the principles of costly obedience and poverty which were to them the hallmark of their calling to be with Christ crucified. What John wrote cannot be properly understood except in the context of the struggles of his life; so that Gerald Brenan's fine recent biography genuinely does augment the *theological* understanding of the English-speaking reader in respect of the saint. To know that – for example – John escaped from prison in Toledo with a notebook containing some of his poetic masterpiece, the *Spiritual Canticle*, which he had composed in his cell, tells us much about how that dense and demanding work is to be read. The emotional intensity of its imagery is to be set against the profound mental suffering which he seems to have undergone at the same time. Brenan (*St John of the Cross: His Life and Poetry*, p. 33) suggests that he 'had some moments of "consolation" ', else he would not have produced such a poem; but the truth is probably subtler. For John, it was fundamentally important to be able to interpret his mental anguish as itself 'grace', the mark of God's intimacy. The *Canticle* becomes more startling than ever if read in such a light; but we shall return later on to a discussion of this. More generally, all of John's work is grounded in the practical – and *political* – struggle to create within his order a style of life authentically reflecting the poverty, the detachment and *disponibilité,* which for him were the central characteristics of Christian 'interior' life.

John had received a thorough education in scholastic philosophy and theology at Salamanca, and his analytical discussions of the spiritual life are couched in the dry terminology of the schools. Yet the most important of these discussions, the long (and incomplete) treatise on *The Ascent of Mount Carmel* (Peers, op.cit., vol. 1), is intended as a commentary on the *Songs of the Soul.* He is a systematic expositor only because he is first a poet; it is the density of meaning in the poems which he felt (and his first readers felt) necessitated elucidation of the sort provided in the prose works. However, the relation here between poetic text and prose commentary is almost absurdly loose: the whole of the prose text discussed only the opening lines of the poem. The relation is closer in the commentary on the *Spiritual Canticle,* but here the interpretation is often awkward and almost mechanical. St John is a sensitive enough poet to be aware that a single image in a lyric may do the work of pages of explication, and a commentary at length on any one line of a poem could equally well be attached to any other. Prose exposition, of its nature, is bound to set out discursively themes which are 'concretized' and compressed in a succession of varying imagistic perspectives in poetry. In other words, the poems do not argue; they reflect, modify and recreate the synthetic vision of experience, which analysis is bound to pull apart and rearrange. But the commentaries remind us that poetry is a precise art: the poems are not emotional outpourings, but theological statements of depth and seriousness. Nor, on the other hand, should the complexity, the dry and technical language of the commentaries be taken to imply that John has an aridly rigorist approach to the life of the spirit. Poetry and prose belong together as much as do reflection and experience in the whole of his life.

The controlling theme of all his writing is one we have already seen to be fundamental for the mainstream of the tradition. God is not the same as anything else. Nothing can 'substitute' for God; once he is tasted by the soul, all earthly or creaturely beauties become tantalizingly inadequate hints and reflections. And the corollary of this for John, as for Aquinas or Gregory of Nyssa, is that when the soul encounters God its 'faculties' do not and cannot operate in their usual way. When the soul is living on this ordinary level, it undergoes intense suffering and frustration, poignantly expressed in some of the Bride's words in the *Spiritual Canticle*:

> Oh who my grief can mend!
> Come, make the last surrender that I yearn for,
> And let there be an end
> Of messengers you send
> Who bring me other tidings than I burn for.
>
> All those that haunt the spot
> Recount your charm, and wound me worst of all
> Babbling I know not what
> Strange rapture, they recall,
> Which leaves me stretched and dying when I fall.
> (Stanzas 6 and 7, tr. Roy Campbell).

John echoes Augustine's attitude to the beauties of creation. God has passed by and touched them (*Canticle* 5), yet his clothing of creation with loveliness serves only to intensify the sense of his own unique, total and inimitable beauty. The Bride looks at the world and sees it, in spite of everything, as speaking of God's absence. Thus, growth in spiritual maturity is growth in detachment from the creaturely. John takes it for granted, as any scholastic would, that a person in some sense *becomes* what he or she loves (see *The Ascent of Mount Carmel* I,iv). So when desire and knowledge are turned towards creatures, the human self is imprisoned. To be determined by knowledge and love of creatures, to have that as the decisive reality of one's inner life, is *not to be able* to know and love God. This may sound drastic; but it is an entirely logical development from the accepted understanding of knowledge with which St John operated. Knowledge unifies, knowledge is participation, in which the knower is moulded to take the form of what is known. And a knowing self cannot at one and the same time take on the form of creatures and the form of the creator; the more truly and intimately God is known, the more weak and remote becomes 'creaturely' knowledge – and vice versa. Thus in its growth 'must the soul be stripped of all things created, and of its own actions and abilities' (*Carmel* II.v; Peers, vol.I, p. 80). It must abandon what is 'its own' – its customary style of acting and experiencing – in order to receive what is God's.

This might suggest a very radical disjunction between nature and grace, or creation and redemption: to be united to God, the soul has to abandon what is 'natural' to it. But this is an over-simple reading. One obvious qualification of it is that John is at pains to affirm God's presence in his creatures; he is present in all souls, as in all created realities, by his sustaining power, without which nothing would have existence. This is the 'natural' union of God and the self. But what is theologically more important is the 'supernatural' union of 'likeness that comes from love' (*Carmel,* ibid.). In other words, the union sought is one of loving relation, and the purification involved is one of fundamental desire. The question put to the believer is about the ultimate direction of his or her life: *for the sake of what* do we live? If the answer to that is in terms of self-directed concern or finite matters in general, the human subject is failing to respond to the deepest vocation of its being, the call to 'likeness' the central paradox that human fulfilment is in going beyond the confines of the self and the tangible world to share the freedom of God; but this should not be confused with the attitude that simply despises or devalues the created order. St John does not seek an 'escape' from creation, but he does regard the purpose of nature as leading towards 'supernature'. The goal of the created order is to point the soul to self-transcendence.

Thus the movement of self or soul is always a stripping, a simplification. And because this means an abandonment of the familiar and secure, it is an immensely costly process. St John of the Cross is normally associated with an almost inhumanly negative and comfortless view of the spiritual life; and it is true that he sets out the human cost of faith with more pitiless candour than almost any comparable writer (even Luther). Yet it is a movement towards fulfilment, not emptiness, towards beauty and life, not annihilation. The night – to use his favourite image – grows darker before it can grow lighter (*Carmel* I.ii; Peers, vol. I, pp. 19–21). It begins with the activity of deliberately 'darkening' the soul, drawing the curtains, so to speak – the liberation of desire itself from external objects and worldly goods. The second and darkest part of the night, the soul's midnight, is the total extinction of any kind of knowledge, leaving only faith and love. And the third part is God's communication of his secrets to the soul; this is also 'night' because what is happening in the soul is indescribable. It should be clear from this that the stages of the 'night' are not simply chronological (as a casual reading of St John might perhaps suggest); essentially they point to three different *kinds* of account of what is happening to the soul in the whole of its life and experience, three levels of 'conversion'. The gradation distinguishing them is one of increasing approximation to the fundamental reality – God's work in the soul.

Yet there is some element here of chronology. Without the 'active' purification of the first night, the night of faith would not exist: it must have its roots in the active life. And only in the forbidding depths of the second night can there be any realization of what it really is for God to give himself to the soul. So John's long and often frankly dull discussion of detail upon relentless detail in the 'active night' has its practical point. He is consciously offering a programme, or at least stating as exhaustively as he can the human preconditions of making God's grace fully your own. The first book of *Carmel* deals for the most part with liberation from ordinary worldly ambition and the desire and hope for material pleasures and comforts (I.iv). John elaborates at some length (I.vi–x) on the suffering and weakness produced in the soul by desire for temporal welfare and success and states with great clarity (xi) why desire for God and desire for worldly good are incompatible. Not all worldly desires are equally harmful; there are temperamental and 'involuntary' matters involved, and, although these are a hindrance to full union, they are not a complete impediment. We have to concentrate first on those things in which we are *free* to choose for or against God – an important point. Yet John sees clearly that the more we advance, the more matters will present themselves to us in these terms of choice for or against God – the almost harmless attachments to places and things, habits that are not gravely sinful, but are still selfish. These, if neglected, will eventually be obstacles as great as any deliberate sin. Once the light of grace shows them as self-orientated, there is no alternative but to struggle for freedom in these things too. 'Upon this road we must *ever* journey' (Peers, I, p. 55; my italics): the price of spiritual freedom is eternal vigilance, and there is no *achieved* and secure freedom to be reached.

The Night of the Spirit

All these details are a test of the authenticity of the soul's conversion. All are forms of the same relentless question which reverberates through the whole of *Carmel:* 'What do you *really* want?' Hence the famous (or notorious) counsels of I.xiii (Peers, p. 61), recommending us always to choose the less congenial way in any decision. Taken out of their context, they read, once again, as impossibly and dehumanizingly negative. But within the discussion of which they are the climax, they have an inescapable logic. The assumption is that what *is* immediately congenial to the self is not in fact directed towards the ultimate fulfilment of the human being: it is trivial and temporary, and so capable of becoming an enslavement. If human desire is met with cheap and momentary gratifications, its proper transcendent directedness is threatened, if not negated. Ascetical practice must involve a *concentration* of desire that can dispense with the ersatz and the comfortable. And of course it should be borne in mind that John sees this as instrumental, not as an end in itself; it should eventually become 'second nature' not to care about gratification – indeed it can be matter for 'delight and consolation' (ibid., p. 42); and this orderly choosing is of more importance than extravagant physical mortifications (I.viii.4;ibid., pp. 42–3).

All this so far has to do with the purification of what John thinks of as the 'sensible' part of the soul – the self in so far as it is conditioned by physical desire and preference. And this is very much a preliminary stage in the soul's advance. John is realistically conscious that it is relatively easy to give up material delights for elevated spiritual pleasures; and it is precisely this area of spiritual satisfaction that the greater part of *Carmel* deals with. The 'night of the senses' is relatively straightforward. The 'night of the spirit' is a deeper and more bitter experience, striking harder at the very roots of illusion and systematically reducing human spiritual activity to the one act of faith and longing. In John's scholastic terminology, the soul has three 'operations', three ways of working – the familiar Augustinian and medieval triad of 'intellect', memory and will or love. Thus, if the whole self is to be brought to God, all these modes must be purified, detached from their determination by finite objects and made empty to receive God. *Carmel* describes the 'active' night of the spirit, the human side of the process: what we can do to identify and interpret this condition, the habits of mind we must cultivate, the dangers we must avoid. The sequel to *Carmel*, the incomplete treatise called *The Dark Night of the Soul*, begins to deal with the 'passive' night, the actual experiential level of God's purifying activity – something, says St John, immeasurably more terrible and costly than the active night alone. It is not just a sequence of decisions to do without spiritual consolation; it is the actual felt absence of consolation, the sense of God as distant, as rejecting, as hostile (the parallels with Luther's *Anfechtung* are clear). So the 'night of the spirit', active and passive, is indeed the 'midnight' that has to come before the dawn. John makes it clear also that this night is, in a special sense, an identification with Jesus and a carrying of his cross (*Carmel* II.vii.7; Peers, pp. 90–1). It is something both simpler and more difficult than 'ways or methods' or any amount of spiritual technique (II.vii.8; ibid., p. 91), and it is incumbent upon every Christian who seriously desires to follow Christ: 'any spirituality that would fain walk in sweetness and with ease, and flees from the imitation of Christ, is worthless' (ibid.).

'Christ is the Way', he is the norm for our 'inner life', and Christ is most totally active for the world's salvation, most completely doing God's work, on the cross, in the depths of his forsakenness, utterly without consolation. It is the climax of the poverty and defencelessness of his whole life: he is brought to nothing, *ad nihilum redactus* (ibid. 9–11; pp. 91–2). If God is to work in us as he wills, we must become Christlike; and that is to bear the 'living death' of inward and outward darkness and lack of consolation. John writes in this section with a marked and rather unusual strength of feeling, acutely aware of the many possibilities of self-indulgence in the Christian soul's approach to the person of Christ. He is not, he makes it clear, writing about those involved in cares and desires of the world, but of those who believe themselves to be devout; if they seek their own gratification in Christ, if Christ becomes instrumental to their self-love, they are as far from Christ as the 'worldly'. 'Christ is known very little by those who consider themselves his friends' (ibid. 12; p. 93).

Christ himself, then, is for John the ultimate touchstone of spiritual 'authenticity' – a point to be remembered by those who regard the historical record of Jesus as tangential to John's 'mystical theology'. It is Christ whose example exposes the dishonesty and selfishness of the 'comforts of religion'. And it is this quality of 'unillusionment', the destruction of fantasies, in the night of the spirit which explains why it is, paradoxically, a part of what theologians have called the 'illuminative way'. It is not simply 'purgation', active or passive, which is the first stage of spiritual growth. It is the beginning of the new level of insight and enlightenment, because the truth about the human relationship with God is, obscurely and confusedly, becoming evident. A modern Carmelite writer has put it with typical depth and clarity:

> Below the level of consciousness we *know* that our pain is the effect of God's closeness; we know it when the pain is withdrawn. We know we have lost for a time that profound companionship which was there in our pain. Such a one as this is more at home in suffering, and it may well be God's providence for them that the night be rarely broken, perhaps only to help them to appreciate its meaning. In suffering they are aware, though not in an emotionally satisfying way, which would neutralize the pain, that they are more in the truth, closer to reality and thus to God. They prefer to feel the utter emptiness of everything, the desolation and the futility of life, rather than be fed with what is not him.
> (Ruth Burrows, *Guidelines for Mystical Prayer*, pp., 101–2).

The same writer goes on to echo St John's point that this is not to be confused with the morbid *desire* for or infliction of suffering; that can become another religious game, another self-generated achievement and security. In this respect, John would agree with Luther that we do not choose or design the particular cross we have to bear. The suffering involved is the pain of not being able to evade the constraints of reality, the 'givenness' of events, understood as coming to us from God's hand: the pain of honesty. Equally it involves the sense of mental confusion or even emptiness so well described by Abbot Chapman. The mind is not occupied with pious or even coherent thoughts: 'The unperceived, infused contemplation occupies the mind, and it can't think of something else; but, as the operation in which it is engaged is either totally or partially imperceptible, the mind seems to be vacant and stupid'

(Chapman, *Spiritual Letters,* p. 88).

And *this* is illumination; not rare mystical trances, visions or ecstasies, but the sense of being drawn into a central, magnetic area of obscurity. Illumination is the running-out of language and thought, the compulsion exercised by a reality drastically and totally beyond the reach of our conceptual apparatus. Illumination is an entry into that 'contradiction' at the heart of Christian belief represented by Jesus on the cross. Thus John insists on the need to let go of cerebral activity when this point is reached. He is writing against a background of assumptions about 'meditation' of a markedly cerebral nature, and when he speaks (*Carmel* II. xiv; Peers, pp. 117–27) of the 'weariness and distaste' produced by meditation, he describes something which a good many other religious of the Counter-Reformation period experienced very intensely (the autobiographical writings of the brilliant Anglo-Welsh convert Benedictine, Augustine Baker, provide a harrowing account of the psychological effects of such meditational techniques as applied in an early seventeenth-century community). John's work is yet another recall from the periphery to the centre, another question to the self-reliance of the manipulative human intellect. What does it matter if 'the mind seems to be vacant and stupid'? The heart is still, imperceptibly, awake to God.

And the life of the heart is not in the ecstatic or the extraordinary. John proceeds to a typically long and careful discussion of what might commonly be regarded as 'illuminative' experiences – visions, 'locutions', clairvoyance (*Carmel* II.xvi – xxxii) – whether imaginative or intellectual, spiritual, supernatural or natural in origin. It is a deliberately devastating catalogue, exhibiting an almost unique sensitivity to the risks of self-deception in the spiritual life. The conclusions are stark: *no* 'spiritual' experience whatsoever can provide a clear security, an unambiguous sign of God's favour. Real knowledge of God cannot be put into words with any approximation to completeness; thus real and personal knowledge of God cannot be identified with words in the understanding (ibid.xxvi; Peers, pp. 194–5). 'Manifestations of knowledge', the passing experiences of wordless intensity and certainty, must be accepted, but not desired or relied upon; so long as they remain transitory, 'accidental' and above all incapable of reduction to verbal formulae, they need not be negatively regarded (ibid., p. 197). As soon as any such thing is turned into a 'mystical experience', to be described and analysed and intellectually 'processed', it will become a delusion. Knowledge of God is thus entirely distinct from knowledge of particulars, of contingent states of affairs, so that clairvoyances about worldly matters, anything that we should now describe as extra-sensory perception, cannot of themselves be proofs or tokens of divine agency. They are at least as likely, for John, to be diabolical (ibid., pp. 202–3). No experience that can be held on to, possessed or comprehended can have to do with God. The characteristic of authentic 'touches of union' is sheer elusiveness.

Similarly, in treating of the way in which feelings (though properly belonging to the 'will') can affect the understanding (ibid.xxxii), John is insistent that nothing must be *done* in connection with them. They are to be accepted passively, not worked on: 'the soul must not strive to attain them or desire to receive them, lest the understanding should itself form other manifestations or the devil should make his entry with still more that are different from them and false' (Peers, p. 223). All this is simply the strict application of *detachment* in every aspect of intellectual life. It may or may not be evident to the understanding what God is doing; what matters is the naked trust in him as present and active, a trust which can only become aware of its own true quality when freed from the supports which are in reality obstacles to truth. John is indeed demanding a kind of abdication on the part of the understanding which strikes at the roots of human self-confidence. Even when you believe you can 'master' a situation intellectually, by setting the usual reasoning activities to work, you *must* refrain where God is concerned. Since intellectual mastery is in fact not possible, and since the intellect is avid for satisfaction, it will almost certainly generate a satisfying falsehood. Thus, satisfaction must be systematically denied it: it must be *reduced* to faith.

Book III of *Carmel* thus begins with a programmatic statement about the purifying of mental and spiritual life; understanding is reduced to faith, memory to hope, will to love (III.i, Peers, p. 225). The rest of the discussion of purgation repeats much of what has been said about the understanding and so is a little more sketchy than Book II. Evidently, John considers the processes connected with memory to be very closely parallel to those he has already written of in II – the stripping away of securities possessed by the mind in so far as it is shaped by forms received from creatures. III.ii,5–8 discusses the disturbances caused in the psyche by the early stages of the memory's purgation and deals with the objection that this sort of disturbance suggests a grace that destroys rather than fulfils nature. What seems to be in question is a rather acute form of the sense of stupidity or vacancy spoken of by Chapman and others; and St John's response is to emphasize that this is characteristic of the preliminary steps because it is at this stage that the strangeness of the psyche's new styles of operating is most intensely felt, and so felt as, not exactly a disruption, but certainly a kind of gap, a shapelessness that is both frustrating and alarming. In the state of union, harmony between 'natural' and 'supernatural' is restored, and grace enables us to perform 'natural' activities as they should be performed (Peers, p. 229). But the first movements towards detachment, being movements away from order, form, structure, 'graspability', will inevitably appear regressive and pointless, a real 'absence of mind' which (as several of Chapman's correspondents seem to have felt) may suggest incipient mental collapse. So, once again, the essential point is repeated: *accept* apprehensions and forms and imaginings and do nothing with them (III.xiii; Peers, pp. 247–9); and accept the attendant bewilderment and frustration as the price to be paid for truth.

The will is purged by growing detachment from the four 'passions' of joy, hope, fear and grief, though only the first is actually treated in *Carmel* (III.xvii-xlv), which was never completed by the saint. Naturally enough, 'joy' demands a very detailed treatment indeed; the word really covers any experience of gratification and so is fundamental for John's whole discussion. There is the now familiar progression from temporal and tangible delights to the subtler satisfactions of morality and spirituality, the ever-increasing astringency. The treatment of rejoicing over moral 'goods' (xxvii–xxix) is particularly valuable as a reminder of the difference between detachment and apathy. John naturally believes that moral rectitude is to be sought and prized and its absence to be lamented; but he is clear that morality isolated from the love of God is pernicious. To be detached from rejoicing over one's own moral probity means to will and to act out of the determination that God shall be served and glorified: to act, that is, from love of God, irrespective of interior satisfaction or external praise. The criterion for action becomes not satisfaction or success, but the compatibility of what we do with the glorifying of God – hence (Peers, p. 295) the need to conceal 'good works' from others and to place no reliance upon them oneself. We are close here to the detachment 'from action and the fruits of action' of the *Bhagavad Gita* – and, at another level, close to that radical scepticism about good works which the Reformers had preached. John's analysis of the dangers of pharisaism is typically sharp and candid. But the point of general significance is, of course, that proper detachment does not necessarily involve an undervaluing of the 'good' concerned; there is no suggestion of sinning so that grace (or detachment) may abound. And this is a valuable corrective for any who would read St John in a purely 'world-denying' sense.

Book III concludes with an unusually fierce succession of chapters about detachment in spiritual matters – a polemic against superstition at all levels. The saint has much to say about the cultus of images and about devotions to particular saints, particular holy places and particular methods of devotion, which will read very strangely to those who share the conventional view of the Counter-Reformation as little more than the matrix of the baroque in art and piety. John's denunciations are a reminder that the Reform itself spoke from and to a centrally 'Catholic' intuition about the risks of idolatry, and that the Counter-Reformation too had its rigorously iconoclastic side. The last enemy to be overcome is religion. Not (of course) that there is any suggestion of that peculiarly modern style of radical Christianity which concludes from this that discipline of life or sacramental observance should be abandoned; for John, as for Luther and so many others, only the Church's discipline could equip the Church's critics. The void of meaning had to be discovered in the heart of the patterns of observance. The relationship between forms, methods and images and the central area of negation and formlessness is always subtle. Form and image are the paths into the night; and John insists that there should be real discernment in their use, so that those should be preferred which genuinely lead away from themselves (III.xxxv; Peers, pp. 311–13). To refuse the question of the *proper* use of form and image, by total indifference (which can characterize both extreme ritualism and extreme puritanism), is to by-pass an essential dialectical moment in the spirit's growth.

Faith and Union

Carmel is professedly an account of 'active purgation', what *we* can do, how *we* can react in clearing the path of God's activity and keeping open a space for him by the exercise of the radical detachment described. It is really advice about how not to impede the work of God. But it does not set out to give a 'programme for attaining perfection', because it does not purport to describe the essential reality of sanctification. The exercise of detachment alone does not purify, it only makes purification possible; and the purification is what *God* does. The mortifications of the 'active night' cannot remove the roots of sin in us. Thus St John begins his continuation of *Carmel, The Dark Night of the Soul,* by an exhaustive catalogue of the imperfections that mortification cannot deal with, and yet another uncomprising warning about the dangers of self-satisfaction. In the words of Ruth Burrows, John 'tells us that the habits of sin are so deeply rooted that only God can destroy them' (op.cit., p. 75). What we must confront at the core of our ascetical struggles is God's frontal assault on the self – something which is, as John says, incomparably more 'horrible and awful' than what has gone before (*Dark Night* I.viii; Peers, vol.I.p. 371). A good many people experience the pains and aridities of *Carmel,* the lostness and shapelessness; relatively few, John suggests, come to the stage of experiencing the 'passive night' in its full weight. The *Dark Night* remains, like *Carmel,* incomplete and is more a series of preliminary warnings, sketches and hints than an analytical account. What seems to be indicated is this: that to experience what God is doing in the soul with any degree of directness involves an acute sense of rejection, humiliation and worthlessness, a sort of dissolution of the sense of *self*; and this is evidently something harsher than the aridity and vacancy of the active night, however painful that may be. This, so John claims, is the necessary prelude to union with God, the final siege of self-defence and self-reliance. It must be remembered that John is not talking about a 'technique' of self-abasement or even a self-devaluing habit of mind, but about the felt consequences of developing closeness with God and the problem of bearing and interpreting these feelings. Once again, we are dealing with the way of *illumination,* strange as that seems: this is a condition in which knowledge is imparted (*Dark Night* I.xii; Peers, p. 387). The difficulty is to separate this knowledge from the intense *emotional* accompaniments of self-loathing, fear and confusion, the sense of abandonment by God, of condemnation to hell (ibid. II.vi; Peers, pp. 409–12). John quotes extensively and movingly from Job, from the Psalter and from some of the prophets in describing the vivid sense of God as enemy and oppressor.

Is this as rare a condition as St John suggests? Perhaps not. The very close similarities with Luther's account of the tension between faith and experience suggest that John's restriction of the experience to 'spiritual proficients' does less than justice to its fundamental role in Christian development, its character as something central to the enterprise of faith itself; though there may indeed be little to suggest that the majority of Christian believers experience anything comparable. It is important to note that John is not discussing a merely 'spiritual' or interior condition. Alienation and dread are produced by all kinds of experiences, by the frustrations and humiliations of daily life; for John himself, the hostility of his brothers and associates, the petty spite with which he was treated in his last months of life, would have been intrinsic to the experience of the passive night. This is still more clear in Augustine Baker, who recommends his readers to be prepared to find the purifying hand of God in the sordid illnesses of old age, in mental disturbances, in the loss of reputation and popularity, in simply finding oneself a nuisance to colleagues or family, and so on. And Ruth Burrows again warns us against supposing that what is in question is a dramatic interior 'mystical' thing:

> What is the essence of your grief, when all is said and done? Isn't it two things; a sense that you lack God, call it absence, call it abandonment, and at the same time a devastating awareness of your own wretchedness? Oh, I know, not in the least like what John of the Cross writes about, that is what you are hastening to tell me, nothing grandiose like that, just drab petty meanness and utter ungodliness. Yes, but that is what he is talking about.
>
> *Guidelines for Mystical Prayer,* p. 88.

That is what he is talking about: the bitter and costly self-knowledge that comes through fear, inadequacy and failure, internal and external, the evaporation of 'spiritual life', the sense of the impossibility of pleasing God, or even of believing in God enough to want to please him: the reduction of spirituality to nothing. The illuminative way; nothing else can serve as a preparation for the authentic union of the self with God.

What can be said of the unitive state is perhaps best left to the saint's own words, most particularly in the later stanzas of the *Spiritual Canticle* and the commentary on them (in vol.II of Peers). But one or two remarks may be made. First, it is clear that John is here dealing with a state in which some sort of direct and joyful experience of God is regularly involved and in which the soul receives insight and knowledge into mysteries. What he does not do, however, is to specify what exactly the experiences are like from a subjective point of view. The sense of God living constantly in the soul, of God's goodness in all things, of the warmth of reciprocal love – all these things of which the *Canticle* speaks at length are described not at all in terms of revelations granted in ecstasy, but in terms of a general dispostion or attitude of the soul, a regular daily mode of seeing and understanding, a new light on things. And if the final chapter of Ruth Burrows' book is accurate and dependable, the state of 'union' is (even more than John perhaps allowed) still compatible with varying *emotional* states. Second, and following on from this: in some respects at least, the state of union involves a re-conversion to creatures. If union is a 'new light on things', it is a fresh sense of the world as God's world, of the continuity as well as the discontinuity between created and uncreated beauty. The soul has 'lofty experience of the knowledge of God, which shines forth in the harmony of the creatures and the acts of God' (*Canticle,* commentary on stanzas XIII and XIV; Peers II. p. 76); and later, the soul desires to see 'the grace and wisdom and beauty which not only does each of the creatures have from God, but which they cause among themselves in their wise and ordered mutual correspondence . . . this is to know the creatures by the contemplative way, which is a thing of great delight, for it is to have knowledge concerning God' (ibid; commentary on stanza XXXVIII; Peers II. p. 180).

To say that knowing creatures in a 'contemplative' fashion is to know God is a point of some considerable significance; it may lead us back to Gregory of Nyssa's insistence that the receptivity of the self before the ungraspable mysteriousness of creatures is not different in kind from the receptivity of the self before God. And perhaps it also looks forward to the theme beloved of Simone Weil, that the practice of selfless attention, self-forgetful attention, to any task is a proper preparation for contemplating God. To be absorbed in the sheer *otherness* of any created order or beauty is to open the door to God, because it involves that basic displacement of the dominating ego without which there can be no spiritual growth.

Why conclude an essay such as this one with John of the Cross? Christian spirituality did not come to the end of its development in 1591, and it seems to beg a serious question if we suggest that everything of real significance had been said by the end of the sixteenth century. That is nonsense, and I have no intention of implying any such view. But what I have sought to show is that St John sums up, in very many respects, those classical themes of Christian spirituality, of the *distincively* Christian understanding of spiritual maturation, without which there can be no fruitful new exploration and articulation of the tradition. John gives exceptionally strong expression to the Christian suspicion of conceptual neatness, of private revelation and religious experience uncontrolled by reference to the giveness of Christ's cross, of infantile dependence on forms and words and images; he accepts the fact that there is a draining and crucifying conflict at the centre of Christian living and refuses to countenance any joy or celebration which has not faced this conflict and endured it. He and Luther are, among the great writers of the Christian past, the most poignantly aware of the ways in which spirituality can be an escape from Christ. For both of them, as for so many others, the test of honesty is whether a man or woman has looked into the darkness in which Christianity has its roots, the darkness of God being killed by his creatures, of God himself breaking and reshaping all religious language by manifesting his activity in vulnerability, failure and contradiction.

The late Cornelius Ernst, OP, argued in two very important papers in *New Blackfriars* (October and November 1969) on 'World Religions and Christian Theology' that the 'genetic moment' of Christian experience, the fundamental novelty of understanding which gives Christianity its identity, 'is at once an experience of the creatively new become manifest in human articulation, and an experience of an ultimate source, the hidden God, *Deus absconditus* who has made his transcendence known in the darkness of a death. If the experience were not *both at once,* it would split apart into an insipid humanism of progress (or a revolutionary arrogance), or an esoteric mystique of world abnegation' (*New Blackfriars,* Nov. 1969, p. 732). This I believe to be the heart of classical Christian spirituality; and these pages have been written out of the conviction that, if we want to discover what Christian identity means historically, we must look at this area of reflection and interrogation that we call 'spirituality' at least as much as we look at the systematic theology which is properly inseparable from it. It is here that we see most clearly the tension in Christian experience between the affirmation of the human and contingent and the devastating rejection of creaturely mediation. On the one hand: the Word is flesh and is communicated in flesh – in historical tradition, in personal human encounter, in material sacrament. The Word re-forms the possibilities of human existence and calls us to the creation of new humanity in the public, the social and historical, world – to the transformation of behaviour and relationship, knowing God in acting and making. On the other hand: the Word made flesh is recognized as such in the great crisis and resolution of crucifixion and resurrection. The Word is rejected and crucified by the world; only when we see that there is no place for the Word in the world do we see that he is *God's* word, the Word of the hidden, transcendent creator. And *then,* only then, can we see, hear, experience (what you will) the newness of that creative God, resurrection and grace, new life out of the ultimate negation and despair. To believe in the newness and the transformation without the rejection and dark is, as Fr Ernst says, insipid and in danger of being cheap; not to believe in it at all is to look for an escape out of this messy world into pure and clear vision, the peace of final negativity. But Christian peace is the peace between the Father and his Son Jesus, person and person together, encounter and gift; it is a peace which *includes* the moment of hopelessness and emptiness, the moment of the cross, and weaves it into life. 'It is the passage', writes Fr Ernst in another work, 'through ultimate negation into the blessed peace beyond the Cross in the exchange of love of Jesus and the Father, the exchange which Christian tradition has called the Holy Spirit. And it is a passage as real as God and as man, as real as Jesus' (*The Theology of Grace,* p. 72).

Christianity begins in contradictions, in the painful effort to live with the baffling plurality and diversity of God's manifested life – law and gospel, judgement and grace, the crucified Son crying to the Father. Christian experience does not simply move from one level to the next and stay there, but is drawn again and again to the central and fruitful darkness of the cross. But in this constant movement outwards in affirmation and inwards to emptiness, there *is* life and growth. The end is not yet; the frustrated longing for homecoming, for the journey's end, is unavoidable. Yet we can perhaps begin to see, through all the cost and difficulty, how we are entering more deeply into a divine life which is itself diverse and moving – Father and Son eternally brought to each other in Spirit. To discover in our 'empyting' and crucifying the 'emptying' of Jesus on his cross is to find God there, and so to know that God is not destroyed or divided by the intolerable contradictions of human suffering. He is one in the Spirit, and in that same Spirit *includes* us and our experience, setting us within his own life in the place where Jesus his firstborn stands, as sharers by grace in that eternal loving relation, men and women made whole in him. In the middle of the fire we are healed and restored – though never taken out of it. As Augustine wrote, it is at night that his voice is heard. To want to escape the 'night' and the costly struggles with doubt and vacuity is to seek another God from the one who speaks in and as Jesus crucified. *Crux probat omnia.* There is no other touchstone. 'I decided to know nothing among you except Jesus Christ and him crucified . . . that your faith might not rest in the wisdom of men but in the power of God' (1.Cor.2.2,5).

A Note on Books

Particularly in the earlier chapters, I have generally made my own translations of texts quoted. In the following list, translations marked with an asterisk are those from which I have made direct quotations. Scriptural quotations are from the Revised Standard Version.

Chapter 1

Three books in particular have shaped a great deal of this chapter:
The Religious Imagination and the Sense of God, by John Bowker (CUP, 1978), *The Crucified is No Stranger,* by Sebastian Moore (London, DLT, 1977), *Suffering,* by Dorothee Sölle (London, DLT, 1976).

Among works on New Testament scholarship, I owe a particular debt to the writings of Professor C. F. D. Moule: most recently, *The Origin of Christology* (CUP, 1977).

Ignatius of Antioch appears in the Loeb Classical Library (vol.I.of *The Apostolic Fathers,* tr. Kirsopp Lake, London, Heinemann, 1930). A good translation is that by C. C. Richardson in vol. I of the invaluable *Library of Christian Classics (LCC): Early Christian Fathers* (London, SCM, 1953).

Chapter 2

On Gnosticism: Hans Jonas, *The Gnostic Religion* (Boston, 1958); and for texts, W. Foerster, *Gnosis: A Selection of Gnostic Texts* (2 vols., Oxford, 1972 and 1974). Also *New Testament Apocrypha**, ed. E. Hennecke, rev. W. Schneemelcher, vol. I. (London, Lutterworth, 1963).

Irenaeus, *Adversus Haereses,* appears in vols. V and VI of the Ante-Nicene Christian Library, tr. A. Roberts and W. H. Rambaut (Edinburgh, 1910). The *Apodeixis* is translated by W. Armitage Robinson (London, SPCK, 1920). On Irenaeus, Gustaf Wingren, *Man and the Incarnation* (Edinburgh, 1959). The works of Philo can be found in the Loeb Library (10 vols., London, 1929 –). Clement's *Quis dives salvetur* and the *Homily to the Newly-Baptized* are translated with the *Protreptikos* by G. W. Butterworth, also in Loeb (London, 1919). The important seventh book of the *Stromateis* is in *Alexandrian Christianity,* an anthology by J. E. L. Oulton and Henry Chadwick (*LCC* II, London, 1954).

This volume also contains Origen's *de oratione, Exhortation to Martyrdom* and *Dialogue with Heracleides.* The *de principiis* is translated by G. W. Butterworth (London, 1936), and the *contra Celsum* by Henry Chadwick (CUP, 1953). The commentary and sermons on the Song of Solomon can be found in the *Ancient Christian Writers (ACW)* series, no. 26, tr. R. P. Lawson (London, Longmans, 1957). Other texts are less accessible; but Jean Daniélou's *Origen* (London, 1955) gives a good deal of valuable quotation and reference and is an excellent introduction.

I have generally referred to the Leipzig edition of Origen's Greek texts (1899 –).

Chapter 3

Athanasius' *contra Arianos, de synodis* and *Vita Antonii* are all included in vol. IV of the *Nicene and Post-Nicene Fathers (NPNF),* tr. A. Robertson (London and Oxford, Parker,

1892); this volume has a good deal of material and excellent notes and introduction.

Vol. v of *NPNF* contains Gregory de Nyssa's *contra Eunomium, de hominis opificio, de virginitate* and the 'Great' catechism, tr. W. Moore and H. A. Wilson (1893). *De beatitudinibus* and *de oratione dominica* are translated by Hilda Graef, *ACW* 18 (1954). The *vita Moysis* has at last been translated in SPCK's new *Classics of Western Spirituality*, by E. Ferguson and A. J. Malherbe (London, 1979). Extensive extracts from this and the homilies on the Song of Solomon appear in the anthology, *From Glory to Glory*, selected with an introduction by J. Daniélou, tr. and ed. by H. Musurillo (London, John Murray, 1962).

For the Greek text, I have used what has so far appeared of the new edn, ed. W. Jaeger (Leiden, Brill, 1960 –); and, for works not yet published in this edition, the Migne *Patrologia Graeca* text.

Some works of Gregory Nazianzen appear in *NPNF* VII (E. H. Gifford, C. G. Browne and J. E. Swallow, 1894). Two of Evagrius' important works are translated by J. E. Bamberger as vol. 4 of the *Cistercian Studies* series: *The Praktikos and 153 Chapters on Prayer* (Cistercian Publications, 1970).

I have also referred to M. F. Wiles, *Working Papers in Doctrine* (London, SCM, 1976) J. Daniélou, *Platonisme et théologie mystique* (Paris, Aubier, 1944); E. Mühlenberg, *Die Unendlichkeit Gottes bei Gregor von Nyssa* (Göttingen, 1966); J. Hochstaffl, *Negative Theologie* (München, 1976).

Vladimir Lossky, *The Vision of God* (London, Faith Press, 1963) has a good chapter on the Cappadocian Fathers. There is, in fact, *very* little in English in this area, though two studies of Basil from the early years of this century have stood the test of time well: W. K. L. Clarke, *St. Basil the Great* (Cambridge, 1913) and E. F. Morison, *St. Basil and his Rule* (Oxford, 1912).

Chapter 4

There is no shortage of good translations of Augustine. Both the *Confessions* and *The City of God* are available in Penguin Classics, the *Confessions* translated by R. S. Pine-Coffin (London, 1961) and *The City of God* by H. Bettenson, with an introduction by David Knowles (London, 1972). The *de Trinitate* is to be found in *LCC* VIII, *Augustine: Later Works,* tr. J. Burnaby (1955). The nineteenth-century Oxford *Library of the Fathers* included a translation of all the *enarrationes in Psalmos* (vols. 24, 25, 30, 32, 37 and 39) into almost unreadable English. The sermons on Pss. 1–37 have been more recently and readably translated by Dame Scholastica Hebgin and Dame Felicitas Corrigan (*ACW*, 29 and 30, 1961).

Latin texts in *Corpus Christianorum (Series Latina)* (Turnhout, 1954 –).

Two indispensable books on Augustine are Peter Brown, *Augustine of Hippo* (London, Faber, 1967) and John Burnaby, *Amor Dei. A Study of the Religion of St. Augustine* (London, Hodder, 1938). I have also referred in this chapter to J. E. Sullivan, *The Image of God; the Doctrine of St. Augustine and its Influence* (Dubuque, 1963).

See also Iris Murdoch, *The Sovereignty of Good* (London, Routledge, 1970).

Chapter 5

The most significant portions of Eusebius' address to Constantine can be found in *Documents in Early Christian Thought,* ed. and tr. Maurice Wiles and Mark Santer (CUP, 1975). Sister Benedicta Ward, SLG, has provided admirable translations of two collections of sayings of the desert fathers, the 'anonymous series' (*The Wisdom of the Desert Fathers,** London, Mowbrays, 1975). *The Letters of St. Antony the Great** have been translated by D. J. Chitty (Oxford, SLG Press, 1975). The *Lausiac History* of Palladius, which gives some of the background to the earliest monastic literature, was translated by W. K. L. Clarke (London, SPCK, 1918), and there is a first-class survey of the whole subject in D. J. Chitty, *The Desert a City* (Oxford, 1966).

The 'Rules' of Basil are included in the *The Ascetic Works of St. Basil,* tr. W. K. L. Clarke (London, SPCK, 1925), and Cassian's *Institutes* and *Conferences* appear in *LCC* XII, *Western Asceticism,* ed. Owen Chadwick (1958). This volume also includes the Rule of St Benedict. Owen Chadwick's essay on John Cassian (CUP, 1950) is still a classic.

I have referred to *Religious Life Today* by J. Coventry and others (Fowler Wright Books Ltd, Tenbury Wells, n.d.), and to *The Monastic Order in England,* by David Knowles (2nd edn, CUP, 1949). In an essay on 'Three Styles of Monastic Reform' in *The Influence of St. Bernard,* ed. Sister Benedicta Ward, with an introduction by Dom Jean Leclercq (Oxford, SLG Press, 1976), I have tried to explore some of Bernard's connections with earlier reformers. The *Cistercian Fathers* series has published translations of many of Bernard's works, including two volumes of *On the Song of Songs,* tr. Kilian Walsh, OCSO (Cistercian Publications, 1971 and 1976), taking the work up to Serm. 46. There is a complete translation by S. J. Eales in *The Life and Works of St. Bernard* (4 vols., London, 1896). *On Loving God* can be found in *Cistercian Fathers* 13, tr. R. Walton (Cistercian Publications, 1973) and in *LCC* XIII, *Late Mediaeval Mysticism,* ed. R. C. Petry (1957). *The Letters of Saint Bernard of Clairvaux** are translated by B. Scott James (London, Burns and Oates, 1953).

The Mabillon text of Bernard is now being superseded by the new critical edn, ed. by J. Leclercq, C. H. Talbot and H. M. Rochais (Rome, 1957 –).

Chapter 6

The only complete translation of Pseudo-Dionysius is by J. Parker (2 vols., London and Oxford, 1897 and 1899). There is also a very idiosyncratic version, by C. E. Rolt, of the *Divine Names* and *Mystical Theology* (London, 1920).

Two works by Maximus are available in English, the *Liber*

asceticus and *Capita de caritate,* translated by Dom Polycarp Sherwood in *ACW* 21 (1955). There is a very important study of Maximus by Lars Thunberg, *Microcosm and Mediator* (Lund, 1965); and I have also referred to Alain Riou, *Le monde et l'église selon Maxime le Confesseur* (Paris, Beauchesne, 1973).

General works which discuss the background of later patristic thought include *The Cambridge History of Later Greek and Early Mediaeval Philosophy,* ed. A. H. Armstrong (CUP, 1967), and two invaluable books by John Meyendorff, *Christ in Eastern Christian Thought* (2nd edn, New Yock, St. Vladimir's Seminary Press, 1975) and *Byzantine Theology* (Fordham University Press, 1974, and London, Mowbrays, 1975).

William of St Thierry, *On Contemplating God,* is in vol. 1 of the *Cistercian Fathers,* tr. Sister Penelope, CSMV (Cistercian Publications, 1970).

For Aquinas, I have used the new Dominican edn of the *Summa Theologiae* (London, Eyre and Spottiswoode, 1964 –). A small collection of Aquinas' writings on prayer is *St. Thomas Aquinas: On Prayer and the Contemplative Life,* ed. H. Pope (London, Washbourne, 1914).

See also: H. John Chapman, *Spiritual Letters,* ed. R. Hudleston (London, Sheed and Ward, 1935, and several times reprinted); D. M. MacKinnon, *The Problem of Metaphysics* (CUP, 1974); Jacques Maritain, *The Degrees of Knowledge* (tr. G. B. Phelan, London, Bles, 1959); and Sebastian Moore, 'Some Principles for an Adequate Theism', *The Downside Review,* July, 1977.

The most extensive translation of Eckhart is that by C. de B. Evans* (2 vols., London, John M. Watkins, 1924 and 1931). This follows the numbering of Pfeiffer's German edn for the sermons, as I have done in this chapter. Translations of Eckhart in the chapter are based on Evans, but clarified and modernized. Two useful smaller collections (with valuable introductory essays) are *Meister Eckhart: A Modern Translation,* by R. P. Blakney (New York, Harper, 1941), and *Meister Eckhart: An Introduction to the Study of his Works with an Anthology of his Sermons,* by J. M. Clark (London, Nelson, 1957). There is also some material in *LCC* XIII, *Late Mediaeval Mysticism.*

Chapter 7

LCC XIII again contains some relevant texts; and the later sections of *LCC* X, *A Scholastic Miscellany,* ed. Eugene R. Fairweather (1956) will give some impression of later scholasticism.

The English mystics are readily accessible: Rolle, Mother Julian and the *Cloud of Unknowing* are all available in Penguin Classics, and an abridgement of Hilton's *Scale of Perfection* by Dom Illtyd Trethowan has recently appeared (the translation is by L. Sherley-Price; London, Chapman, 1975).

LCC XV–XVIII provides a good assortment of Luther texts. XVI *(Early Theological Works,* ed. and tr. J. Atkinson, 1962) has the Heidelberg Disputation, XVII (*Luther and Erasmus: Free Will and Salvation,* ed. and tr. E. G. Rupp, A. N. Marlow, P. S. Watson and B. Drewery, 1969) includes *The Bondage of the Will,* and XVIII is the collection of *Letters of Spiritual Counsel** (ed. and tr. T. G. Tappert, 1955).

B. L. Woolf's two volumes of *Reformation Writings of Martin Luther** (London, Lutterworth, 1952 and 1956) contain several shorter works, including *The Freedom of a Christian* (The Liberty of a Christian Man). G. Rupp and B. Drewery, *Martin Luther**, in the *Documents of Modern History* series (London, Edward Arnold. 1970) is an excellent anthology.

W. von Löwenich, *Luther's Theology of the Cross,* has been translated by H. A. Bowman (Belfast, Christian Journals Ltd, 1976). E. G. Rupp, *The Righteousness of God* (London, Hodder, 1953) is indispensable. G. Wingren, *The Christian's Calling* (tr. C. C. Rasmussen, Edinburgh, 1958) is an important and stimulating essay by this major Swedish theologian.

A valuable general survey is G. Ebeling's *Luther: an Introduction to his Thought* (London, Collins, 1970). Biographies include R. Bainton's popular *Here I Stand* (London, Hodder, 1951), and the more scholarly *Martin Luther: A Biographical Study,* by J. M. Todd (London, Burns and Oates, 1964).

Regin Prenter's article on 'Holiness in the Lutheran Tradition' in *Man's Concern with Holiness* (ed. M. Chavchavadze, London, Hodder, 1970), is an admirable discussion of major themes.

Chapter 8

Probably the best complete translation (with excellent notes and introductions) is E. Allison Peers, *The Complete Works of St. John of the Cross** (3 vols., London, Burns and Oates, 1934–5). The poems are memorably rendered by Roy Campbell (*The Poems of St. John of the Cross**, with preface by M. C. D'Arcy, London, Harvill, 1951). There is also a translation of the poems by Lynda Nicholson in Gerald Brenan's *St. John of the Cross: His Life and Poetry* (CUP, 1973).

E. W. T. Dicken, *The Crucible of Love* (London, DLT, 1963) is a major critical and comparative study of John and Teresa; and Edith Stein, *The Science of the Cross* (London, Burns and Oates, 1960) is an interpretation of John by one who was herself a figure of the greatest spiritual significance. At a more introductory level, E. A. Peers, *Spirit of Flame* (London, SCM, 1943 – very recently reprinted) can be warmly recommended.

I have made extensive use of Ruth Burrows, *Guidelines for Mystical Prayer* (London, Sheed and Ward, 1976). Cuthbert Butler, *Western Mysticism* (2nd edn, London, Constable, 1926) is brilliant and wide-ranging, but its judgements on St John are to be treated with great caution.

The late Fr Cornelius Ernst, OP, left only a few published books and papers, but their importance is quite out of proportion to their size. I have been very much influenced by 'World Religions and Christian Theology' (*Multiple Echo*, Darton, Longman & Todd, 1979) and *The Theology of Grace* (Fides Publishers Inc., Notre Dame, Indiana, 1974 – no. 17 in the *Theology Today* series).

Index of Names and Titles